The Book on Increasing Your ROI

How to Obtain Huge Profits in the Manufactured Home Market

Lori Robinson

The Book on Increasing Your ROI: How to Obtain Huge Profits in the Manufactured Home Market

©2017 Lori Robinson

ISBN: 978-1772770544

www.thebookonincreasingyourroi.com

Published by
10-10-10 Publishing
Markham, Ontario
CANADA

Contents

Contents

This book is dedicated to my sister,

Debbie Guernsey,

*whose spiritual support and daily encouragement
gave me the incentive to write this book
and accomplish even more.*

Acknowledgments

It is with deep gratitude I would like to thank the following for what each has done to enrich my life:

To God, with whom all things are possible,

To my husband and lifelong friend, Dean Robinson, who was the first to say I had a book inside me and supported me, in whatever way I needed to get this book done, and whose organization skills have been essential to my success, who is my rock, who is always by my side, cheering me on in Real Estate and supporting me in all the other endeavors in our life together,

To my children Brittany, Heather and Steve, whose support is always felt and are always there when I need them, and who somehow thought I was amazing, when I thought I was just a mom,

To my sister Cindy, who was my best friend when we were growing up, and whose positive competitive spirit, allowing her to exceed in business and athletics, has been an inspiration to me,

To my mom, Darlene Guernsey, who taught me that God loves me and guides me, and to my dad, Frank Guernsey, who would have really enjoyed learning about making money in the manufactured home market,

To my friend Diane Cihangir, who has supported me in deep friendship, as our children grew up together, always hanging out in each other's homes, and whose dedication to transcribing almost my entire book in only a couple days made finishing this book possible,

To my daughter in law, Kristin Robinson, who enthusiastically, efficiently and effectively went through every word and sentence in this book with a fine tooth comb, and whose artistic talents and intelligence I admire in so many areas,

To Raymond Aaron, who made this book a reality, through his 10-10-10 program, and who has provided me with words of wisdom for several years,

To Liz Ventrella, who helped me many times when I needed help executing different aspects of Raymond's program,

To Cara Witvoet, my book architect, who pushed me over the finish line,

To Chris Foss, who patiently designed and redesigned my website, and whose many talents I admire,

To Jerry and Kathleen Foss, from Foss Studios, who took great care in providing a comfortable atmosphere, for taking my photo for the back cover of this book, and whose friendship is so appreciated,

To Jim Stehlik, who mentored me in mobile homes and other Real Estate investing ventures and through whose wisdom I was able to continue making a difference in people's lives by placing them in the American Dream they could afford, and who also took the time to send in an example of a mobile home deal to be included in the last chapter of this book,

To Christy Duckett-Harris, who, even though I called her out of the blue, was kind enough to take the time to send in an example of a mobile home deal to be included in last chapter of this book and whose example of how she does business I want to emulate,

To Greg Downing, whose inspiration opened my eyes and triggered my plunge into the world of Real Estate investing,

To Michael Poggi, founder of The Millionaire's Group, an international investment company, whose wisdom about using self-directed Roth IRAs and ideas about investing in Real Estate have helped me immensely, whose respect for the people he invests with I admire, and who lives by example what he teaches,

To Nathan Long and Nate Hare from Quest IRA who shared with me the power of self-directed Roth IRAs and the importance of investing in what I believe in,

To Jonathan Dugger, who taught me by example, practicing what he teaches about investing in mobile homes,

To my friends at Chicago Area Real Estate Investment Association, especially Ben Walhood, Rob Hayes, Chris Leon and Mark Imburgia, with whom I have had many enjoyable Cash Flow game nights and who provided awesome informational and networking opportunities,

To John and Janelle Swiercinsky, who taught me: "Your net worth = your network", by throwing lots of parties, including a surprise birthday party for me. Thank you! Also, who took the time to teach others what they know and were transparent about their Real Estate practices, and also for starting Chicagoland Real Estate Connections Club, where I have met many new friends,

To Chad Barker, who gave me great advice on how to talk with the investors financially supporting my deals, and who also gave me advice on how to take control of a deal,

To the late Lonnie Scruggs, the original "Lonnie dealer" who paved the way for many others to do mobile home deals through his book: "Deals on Wheels",

To Frank Rolfe and Dave Reynolds from Mobile Home Park University who gave me insights into the running of mobile home parks and created a means for me to reach other "Lonnie dealers",

To Mark Lindberg, who brings me ice cream and always asks me about my next sweet deal,

To Adam Duvel, my fellow investor, whose expertise in Real Estate I value and whose encouragement I appreciate,

To Jim Bratko, who was the first person to introduce me to others as a Real Estate investor,

To John Barnak, who introduced me to a network of local Real Estate investors,

To Jeff Jewel, who has shared his knowledge of Real Estate with me and opened his Realty office at Inspire Realty Partners to play the game Cash Flow,

To Paul Comino and his sons Kyle and Joel, who through their lifetimes of experiences in mobile homes, have taught me nuances in the business of buying and selling of mobile homes and mobile home parks,

THANK YOU!

Foreword

Do you want a check in the mail every month from someone you provided the American Dream for? Lori's book, *The Book on Increasing Your ROI: How to Obtain Huge Profits in the Manufactured Home Market*, shows you how her WINning approach to the manufactured home market can systematically increase your return on investment. Her unique program finds 'Who's In Need', and provides you a solution to meet the need, resulting in making a profit for you. She details step by step, how to increase your ROI by investing in mobile homes. Lori's deep desire is to help you give those in need, who thought they could never own a home at an affordable price, the American Dream. This will create a significant profit for you as the investor. Through her exclusive investment approach, explained in this book, Lori demonstrates how you can double your initial investment in approximately 4 years, leading to at least 100% ROI. Wow!

When I first met Lori several years ago at a workshop that I was hosting in Chicago, I could tell that she was looking for something new in her life and this is what led her to write this very book. I could see that she was a very compassionate and determined person. Being a dedicated mom and leader in her community, Lori is passionate about teaching and helping you.

Lori was drawn to Real Estate for years, but she did not want to be a Realtor, a career that her parents and grandparents had pursued. It was the peak of the great recession. There were boarded up houses, begging to have families live in them, all over the city where she lived. Many lessons were learned through the first rental home she and her husband owned, including how to evict tenants. This was Lori's beginning step to the real estate world, which led her to realize a much higher ROI was to be had, investing in mobile homes. Lori shares her experiences and real life investments, both successful and unsuccessful, in order to teach you how to avoid the same mistakes she made and lessons that she learned through her experiences.

What is admirable about Lori is that she uses negative experiences, like the rental house mentioned above and a mobile home deal that did not work, which she discusses in detail in her book, to propel her forward. That's why I say she is determined.

Lori is the kind of person who would go out of her way to help you; whether you are a friend, family member or stranger. That's what she is doing now; she is helping you to jump-start lives by turning lifelong renters into homeowners, making you a hefty profit.

I endorse this book as a must read as Lori can help you to increase your ROI. In doing so, you fulfill the dreams of lifelong renters to become homeowners, while increasing your income.

Raymond Aaron
New York Times Best Selling Author

Introduction to WIN

The WINning approach to the manufactured home market that systematically makes you money!

Are you ready to find out how to obtain huge profits in the manufactured home market? Skeptical, aren't you? I was when I first heard about it. It is not a usual way to invest, therefore it must be risky. Or so we are told. Having a systematic approach reduces risk. This book is about how my WINning approach to the manufactured home market can systematically make you money. How? I will get to that soon, but first I'll talk about where the money you have goes, and the risks and rewards of the most popular investments.

If you are like most Americans, you have a steady paycheck. You work hard, at least 40 hours a week and often 60 or more. You might even invest already or have an investment portfolio with a stock broker.

But who has money for investments when, according to credit.com, the average American owes about $7,000 in credit card debt, $10,000 in auto loans and $100,000 in a mortgage? The average student owes $25,000 in student loans. Fourteen percent of Americans put 40% or more of their paycheck into credit card payments, so what is left to invest? These debts can be paid off by paying more than the minimum on at least one credit card every month and as that one is paid off, use that money to pay off the other credit cards one by one. That method may help you get out of debt, and there are other methods as well which are out of the scope of this book, but the point is that even if you are in debt, you can make money. More on how this can be done will come later in this chapter.

You may not be like most Americans. You may be completely out of debt. Is your money, the money you earn working hard all week, really working for you? If you invest, whether you are in debt or not, how risky are your investments? What kind of an impact do your investments have on others? Do your investments reflect your values? What is your ROI? How long will it take you to double your money? These are important questions to consider when investing.

There is a formula called the Rule of 72 that calculates an approximation of when an investment, using compound interest, doubles. It will be referred to through the rest of this chapter. This is the formula.

72 / interest rate = years to double

Let's take a look at some of the most popular investment vehicles: money markets, mutual funds, stocks, IRAs, CD's and passbooks.

According to Bankrate.com, the average money market account annual yield at the writing of this book, April 2016, was 0.26% with the best money market at 1.00%. So if you have, let's say, $100,000 to invest, how long will it take to double your money? Using the Rule of 72, it will take 72 years at 1% annual return (72/1 = 72), and with a 0.26% yield, it will take about 277 years to double your money (72/0.26 =276.92). That is too long. Who has 72 years to wait for money to double? No one has 277 years for money to double. Although Money markets are very stable investments and very liquid investments, they do not produce a very high yield.

Mutual funds are a portfolio of stocks picked by the experts that you trust, hired to give you the best return with the least amount of risk. During the stock crash of 2008, stocks crashed by 40-50%. So lots of people who were depending on their investments for a nest egg, for a child's college education, for medical bills or even just for a rainy day, lost a lot of money. That doesn't look very stable. Mutual funds and stocks sound very risky and not very profitable, when looked at it from this perspective, yet this is the most "stable" investment vehicle most people use. What do your mutual funds invest in? A prospectus is sent every year to anyone investing. Have you ever read it? Do the stock choices in your mutual funds reflect your values? I was listening to a veteran one day talk about the mutual fund he once had invested in. He contacted the company to ask what specifically the company invested in. He was told it varied from day to day, depending on what the experts thought would give their clients the best yields. So, he pushed the issue. He asked: "What are you investing in today?" Finally, after several phone calls, he received a list of companies this mutual fund invested in. One of them made this man's heart sink. On the list was the company: Bin Laden Construction. As a veteran he was horrified to learn he had been investing in Bin Laden Construction. It was against everything he believed in. As a result, he started his own investment company offering self-directed IRAs, encouraging others to invest in what they believe in, not just what the experts say will produce the best yield. If you work hard for your money, don't you want to invest in something you believe in?

Let's talk about stocks. A lot of people like to play the market. Note how that is worded, "play the market". It already sounds like gambling. According to a friend of mine, a former very successful stock broker, who has a wall full of awards showcasing his accomplishments as a stock broker, says that is exactly what investing in the stock market is--a gamble. He compares playing the stock market to going to Vegas. Every investment portfolio will say the words: "Past performance is not necessarily indicative of future results", because it is not. He has told me and lots of other people about how when he was a stock broker, he and other members of his company were often wined and dined into promoting a particular stock. And they did. When my friend's boss said, "We are promoting company X today," all the stockbrokers got on the phone and promoted company X, artificially inflating the market and everybody won--or did they? Did the stock increase because the company was doing better or did the company stock do better because demand had increased? We'll never know. This man, Michael Poggi, is now an author and national speaker and also founder of The Millionaire's Group, where he educates people on how to buy Real Estate and other investment vehicles, ideally using a self-directed Roth IRA. He makes money with his clients, not off them. The stock market can be wild. According to CNN Money (December 31, 2015), 70% of investors lost money in the stock market last year. You can win a fortune, or lose your shirt, which is why many people invest in mutual funds, to reduce risk, but we've already seen that is not very profitable and it's risky. What system can be depended on to ensure a higher return and a lower risk?

Over 7 trillion dollars are invested in IRAs and 401ks in America. Most invest in mutual funds and stocks, which have been established to be low yielding, risky and possibly not reflective of your values. Do you wish you had a higher yielding, less risky financial vehicle to invest in? In this book, you will be learning about a little known niche market that meets the needs of millions of Americans and puts money in your pocket month after month.

Placing your money in a self-directed Roth IRA can be a wise choice, and there will be more detail on that later in this chapter, because it can be an advantageous way to invest in the manufactured home market.

CDs, or Certificates of Deposit, are generally considered to be safe investments. In this case, safe means that they are FDIC insured up to $250,000. At this time, CDs with terms of 1-5 years yield between 1% and 2% annually, depending on the terms and the minimum deposit. Using the Rule of 72, you could double your income in 36 years. That is most of your working years. You can do better.

Passbooks or checkbooks are another generally accepted safe investment; however, their yield is very low. They vary in their rate of return, but rarely go above 1% and can go as low as 0.06%. So, according to the Rule of 72, they take between 72 and 1200 years to double in value. They are safe, protected by the FDIC; and if you use a local bank, they invest in building your own community. But, not only do these take way too long to double, they are making less that the average inflation rate each year. You can do a lot better.

Maybe a nonconventional investment is a good idea. How about investing in Real Estate? What about trying a fix and flip? It's all the rage on TV. Some say you could be earning $20,000- 40,000 per house. Why not try it? Without the proper education and experience, fixing and flipping houses could lose you, or someone who invests in you, a lot of money. Most fix and flips need at least $200,000 in acquisition and repair costs. That's a lot of money to risk if you don't know exactly what you are doing. There are two approaches to this type of investment, the hands on and the hands off approach. In a hands on approach, you do as much as you can yourself and hire out for those things you cannot do. You can use your own or other people's money. The hands off approach, sometimes called the armchair investor approach, involves you handing someone else your money and hoping for the best. It's all about systems. What systems are in place? What questions did you ask? How well do you or the person you are investing with know your stuff?

Let's say you decide to do everything yourself and you are using someone else's money. Can that person afford to lose that money if something goes terribly awry? Why should that person trust you? By the end of this book, you should know enough to be confident investing in the manufactured home market where the risks and initial investments are lower, providing your investor with possibly a 10% annual return, and earning money for yourself without investing any of your own money. (It is recommended that you partner with an experienced investor for at least your first deal to minimize risk - and one needs to minimize risk as much as possible). Can you afford to risk someone else's money in a real estate fix and flip, where the risks and initial investments are much higher than a manufactured home without proper training or experience? Can you crunch numbers to see what house is a good deal to buy, what the buy/sell margin needs to look like, how much repairs cost, just by looking at the house? Can you, or someone you know, do: roofing, electrical, plumbing, HVAC, hot water heaters, foundations and structural, carpentry/ cabinetry, landscaping, driveways, drywall, painting, flooring, staging – all within your margins and without losing money? Do you know how to remove junk from a property? Not everything can go into a dumpster. Once, in a house I was working on, a former resident who had passed on left an oxygen tank behind. Ultimately, it got taken to the fire station. Who would have thought that's where it goes? Can you deal with mold, pest infestation or adding a second story in order to keep up with the recently upgraded neighborhood? Do you know how to deal with contractors, contracts, and setting up reasonable time tables for completions so as not to lose money? Do you know how to deal with hard money lenders? Do you know how to price your home once it is completed so it doesn't stay on the market too long? And there are many, many more decisions to make from start to finish. Many rehabs are a 4-6 month commitment. Is your time, money, and frustration really worth the risk of possibly making money or losing your money or a significant amount of someone else's money? Too risky! The return could be high--but it is only for 6 months. You will have to invest more money to do it again, so you can't really calculate how long to double your money with the Rule of 72, since the money is being reinvested each time.

Maybe you want to be an armchair investor and you have a friend, a handyman, who wants to flip a house, but wants you to provide the money. Do you have enough confidence in your friend's knowledge and experience to be confident he can make money for you? Is this person an expert in his field? What can you base this on? Do you know what questions to ask and, more importantly, do you know what the answers should be? What looks good on TV may be more risky than first thought. Those people on TV make it look easy. But, like a duck that looks like it is smoothly swimming quickly through the water, he is paddling like the dickens underneath. A flip is a lot of work.

Another Real Estate option might be buying a house and renting it. Why not? Lots of people do it. Become a landlord. Do you have the education and experience in every aspect of doing rentals to be a landlord? Are you using other people's money? Can those people afford to lose the money if something goes awry? Why would someone trust you if you have never done this before? Do you know the factors to take into consideration in order to determine the most money you will spend on the purchase of the home so that there is an appropriate margin between monthly total expenses of owning the home and the rental income? Do you know how to crunch numbers for this deal? If you charge too high a rent, no one will be interested. If you charge too little a rent, you will get too many applicants. Let's say you buy a house for $100,000 and rent it for $1000/mo. That looks great. A 12% return. Oh, maybe not. That's your gross income, not your cash flow. If you paid cash for the house, then you would not have a mortgage but you will still have to pay for insurance, taxes and (hopefully only) minor maintenance. So for round numbers let's say taxes are $400/month and insurance and minor maintenance is $100. Let's assume for this example that you will be doing your own management. So now your ROI is 6%. That's ok. It's still better than a money market. Rule of 72 says, 12 years to double your money. Nice,--until the hot water heater bursts or the roof needs replacing or the furnace stops working or the basement floods or a number of any other problems. That will definitely reduce your ROI. But, what if no major maintenance problems happen? You could receive cash flow month after month, except for when you don't, because some drama happened and your tenants snuck out in the middle of the night and you are left with the trash, animal waste all over the floor, utility bills that have not been paid, the missing appliances etc., etc. Now you have no income, negative cash flow, a big hassle on your hands and your ROI is negative.

Maybe your buddy wants to hassle with all of the above, if you just chip in the down payment and take on the mortgage to invest in the rental house. Once again, ask; do you have enough confidence in someone else to make the money for you? What can you base this on? Is this person an expert in his field? Does he have a track record for making money in rentals? Do you know the questions to ask him and enough right answers to be able to make an educated decision to trust your money for rental income property to your buddy? So your ROI for rentals could be from 0-12%, and without education and experience your ROI could very possibly be negative.

There are speculative investments that could return a very hefty ROI, or you could lose your principal, but that is why they are called speculative--they are a gamble. Sometimes the person asking for your money has reason to believe that the oil well will gush or that the gold mine will pan out or that start-up company will make money, but it is speculative. It is too much risk.

One way to increase your return is to use a self-directed Roth IRA. Why? Because no matter how you invest, whether personally or using your LLC, you will be taxed on your gains, whereas if you invest directly from your self-directed Roth IRA, your money was already taxed and cannot be taxed again as income. Let's say for example that you converted $133,000 from your 401K or regular IRA to a self-directed Roth IRA, paid your gains and penalties of $33,000 (just an estimate - every tax situation is different) which is an initial major ouch to your wallet. Now you have $100,000 to invest, which you can double in four years to $200,000, without being taxed again, using your self-directed Roth IRA. Not only can you invest from your self-directed Roth IRA, you can loan money from your Roth IRA. You can borrow from your self-directed Roth IRA. It is its own entity. You cannot be taxed again on income earned within the self-directed Roth IRA. You can see that the tax implications here are fantastic. If you have never heard of a self-directed Roth IRA before, look into it, but be wary, because some companies will claim they are self-directed but they are not. These companies may say to you that they are self-directed, and then give you a choice of what stock portfolio or mutual fund you want to choose from. This is not self-directed. There are many more choices as to what you can invest in. A self-directed Roth IRA can invest in Real Estate, businesses and, yes, even manufactured housing.

Quest IRA is the company that was formed by the veteran I mentioned earlier. The people at this company are very transparent and honest and they place how you self-direct your Roth IRA in your hands, while also providing education as to how investing with a self-directed IRA works and the documents needed for you to do so. There are many other good providers out there too. This information is being included in the introduction of the book because this information alone could save you thousands of dollars.

Some people accept roadblocks to increasing their ROI. They say they do not have enough time or money to invest. These obstacles can be combated, and will be discussed further in Chapter One. The key is to learn more. Throwing more money at investments does not increase your ROI, but increasing your knowledge of how each investment works can increase your ROI. With proper knowledge, you will choose your investments wisely, you will understand what your money is really being invested in, how your investment impacts others, and what your real ROI is, and you will WIN.

What is **WIN**? It is finding **W**ho's **I**n **N**eed, providing a solution to meet that person's need and winning (profiting). Throughout this book, I will examine how you can meet the needs of yourself and others and WIN.

Is it possible to double your money in just a few short years? Is it possible to receive large returns with less than a $10,000 investment?

Is it possible to see returns higher than flipping a house? Is it possible to receive high returns month after month for four years straight? Is there an investment out there that does all of this and gives hard working Americans the opportunity to have the American Dream they would have never thought was possible? Yes! It is possible. This niche market is the manufactured home market. How high of an ROI can you get? The first chapter starts with an example of over 100% ROI and then explains step by step how you can do this too, or understand enough about the market to invest in someone with experience.

#1

YOU WIN!
Who's In Need (WIN) of monthly cash flow and most excellent ROI? You are!

You can make money in the manufactured home market even if time or funds are lacking. You can get a check in the mail month after month after month.

Are you in need of a higher return on your investments? That's what this book is about, increasing your ROI. Ideally, you want your investments to work for you, so you don't have to. Sometimes, you may want to buy stuff, so although I spoke of other investment vehicles in the introduction, I am beginning this first chapter with a comparison of buying something cool you might really want and, of course, since this book is about increasing your ROI in the manufactured home market, I am comparing the ROI of that purchase to the purchase of a manufactured home. The manufactured home, described in the following example, is one I actually bought and brings income to my mailbox month after month.

Let's say that you have $10,000 in your pocket, just burning a hole in there. Here are two options of something that you could buy: a TV or a manufactured home. Let's calculate the ROI, the return on investment on both over four years.

$$ROI = \frac{(Revenue\ from\ Investment - Cost\ of\ Investment)}{Cost\ of\ Investment}$$

You can buy the most awesome TV on the market, which when I last looked it up was a $10,000.00 78 inch Curve 4KSUHS Smart TV. So you buy the TV to deck out your entertainment room, and over the next four years it earns no money for you. At the end of four years, if it still works at all, it is no longer the latest and greatest and is worth a tiny fraction of what you paid for it. You decide to give it away.

$$ROI\ of\ \text{"awesome"}\ TV = \frac{\$(0 - 10,000)}{\$10,000} = \frac{-\$10,000}{\$10,000} = -1.00$$

$$= -100\%\ ROI\ over\ the\ course\ of\ four\ years$$

Your return on investment is negative 100%.

Perhaps, even though you have the cash, you decide to charge the TV. Larger purchases are often charged. Let's say you put it on your credit card at 7% because you have pretty good credit, and let's say you take 4 years to pay off this TV. So you put $10,000 on your credit card and you get to watch that totally awesome TV in your man cave for 4 years.

But it is not just going to cost you $10,000, it is going to cost you $10,000 plus 7% APR. Over the next four years you will incur interest charges which will vary tremendously depending on how much you pay each month. You might wind up paying $1500-2300 in interest over four years. Of course, it will vary depending on whether you pay it off a little each month and all at the end or whether the interest rate varies or any other number of factors. The point is, while you are watching your football team almost make it to the super bowl for four years, your TV is making you no money at all. It just sits there in the corner of the room losing you money day after day, month after month, and year after year. That TV, that is the envy of all your friends, is a liability--not an investment.

$$ROI \ of \ "awesome \ TV = \frac{\$(-2,300 - 10,000)}{\$10,000} = \frac{-\$12,300}{\$10,000} = -1.23$$

$-123\% \ ROI \ over \ the \ course \ of \ four \ years$

Your return on investment is negative 123%.

Or... you could take that same $10,000 and buy yourself a 3 bedroom 2 bath 1100 square foot mobile home. This is not a down payment; this is cash for the full purchase of the mobile home. (Yes, these mobile homes do exist. Look on the internet at Craigslist or MHVillage or MHBay in your area under "manufactured housing".) Then, you could resell that mobile home to someone else for $20,000 with seller finance over a 4 year period and you could charge this new buyer (sometimes called the end buyer) anywhere from 0% to 18% interest, depending on your investor's needs and the financial risk of the end buyer. Now what do you have after 4 years? Unlike the TV example, you don't own the manufactured home, but you do possess a lien on a manufactured home, which means you have a promissory note that says the person living in the manufactured home (the owner) will make monthly payments to you every month for four years. The person living in the mobile home owns the mobile home. He is responsible for anything that goes wrong in the mobile home. Unlike the purchase of the TV, this expenditure produces a check in your mailbox month after month after month for four years, instead of a bill. Your responsibility is to cash the check.

At 10% interest, amortized over 4 years to the end buyer (a $507.25 monthly payment), you have a total revenue of $24,348, a 143 % ROI over the four year loan period.

At 18%, amortized over 4 years (a $587.50 monthly payment), that is a total revenue of $28,200, a 182% ROI over the life of the loan. So at the end of 4 years, you have between $24,348 and $28,200 in your pocket, enough to buy another manufactured home or a brand new fancy TV or money for a vacation and some left over!

$$ROI \text{ on manufactured home @ } 10\% = \frac{\$(507.25 \text{ x } 48) - \$10,000}{\$10,000}$$

$$= \frac{\$24,348 - \$10,000}{\$10,000} = \frac{\$14,348}{\$10,000} = 1.43 = 143\% \, ROI$$

$$ROI \text{ on manufactured home @ } 18\% = \frac{\$(587.50 \text{ x } 48) - \$10,000}{\$10,000}$$

$$\frac{\$28,200 - \$10,000}{\$10,000} = \frac{\$18,200}{\$10,000} = 1.82 = 182\% \, ROI$$

That is one heck of a return on investment! And it is possible. The money invested in the manufactured home works for you. That is what money should do! Let's increase your ROI in the manufactured home market.

You may have a lot of questions. Let's start with some basics. So, how exactly do you picture a manufactured home or what is also referred to as a mobile home? They are interchangeable terms. Manufactured home sounds a little bit nicer, but a bit cumbersome.

Does the term mobile home bring the pictures below to mind?

The homes above are rusted through. The roofs are sagging. The decks are not stable at all. Grass, and other foliage, is growing up around the mobile homes. There is random stuff lying outside the mobile homes. I provide decent affordable housing for hard-working Americans. The above pictures are not examples of what I provide. I am not a slum lord. Sadly, people were living in these mobile homes. When I speak of mobile homes throughout the rest of the book, picture the mobile home below, not the ones above.

Here is a picture of the mobile home I described in the example of the ROI comparing the purchase of a manufactured home to the purchase of a TV:

This is the mobile home that I bought for $10,000, a beautiful 3 bedroom 2 bath, 1100 square foot, well maintained home. The end buyer made it look even more beautiful.

So how much does a mobile home cost? The mobile home you see above was purchased for $10,000. Mobile homes can range anywhere from $1 to $160,000, sometimes even higher. One dollar for a mobile home? It's true, but not very common. Sometimes, the owner is just trying to give away his home. Just this week, I was offered to buy a mobile home for one dollar. It was a functioning 2 bedroom /1 bath mobile home, approximately 1000 square feet with two wooden decks and a beautiful garden. It needed a new bathroom sink and new windows. The owner bought a regular house and did not want to continue to pay for lot rent along with his new mortgage. Before I developed this system, I almost got to the point of giving away a mobile home as well. I will discuss the lessons learned from purchasing that mobile home in the next chapter.

All of the mobile homes shown so far are single wide mobile homes. Single wide homes range from approximately 600-1100 square feet in size. These homes get transported from the manufacturer to the mobile home park on one tractor trailer. There are also double wide, triple wide and even quadruple wide mobile homes, requiring that number of trucks. Triple and quadruple wide mobile homes are 2000+ square feet or bigger and look like a regular house. They generally have an attached garage. Just like a single wide, these mobile homes have a skirt around their base and no basement. Mobile homes can be placed on a foundation. When placed on a foundation, they are usually considered Real Estate because they are attached to the land. The mobile homes I deal with are not on foundations; they are on piers or cinderblocks, in mobile home parks. The park owns the land and the homeowner owns just the mobile home itself. Although most mobile homes will never move once brought from the manufacturer, under their skirts, they all have wheels and can be carried away by a tractor trailer. Most of the newer mobile homes that you see will be between $40,000 and $60,000, but most of the ones that I purchase cost between $3,000 and $10,000. So why should you or I invest in mobile homes? Little by little, from the introduction of the book until now many reasons have been stated as to why you should invest in mobile homes. But the bottom line is that you can at least double your money in 4 years and if you follow this system, you will have money in your mailbox every month. Also, by in investing in mobile homes, you are providing the American Dream to people who may not have thought it was possible.

Many people in America live in mobile homes. Many more people could live in mobile homes if they could see that they could afford it. Investing in the mobile home market is a narrow niche market, but is much needed. More explanation on why you are so needed investing in this market can be found in the chapters on buyers and sellers. The bottom line is that those individuals who wish to purchase a mobile home to live in cannot always depend on the banks for their needs in the manufactured home market.

Mobile homes are neither real estate nor generally mobile. Details as to what they really are will be covered in a later chapter. Once a mobile home gets to its destination at a mobile home park, often it stays there for 10, 20, 30 years, usually until it is no longer useful as a mobile home. Many of the mobile homes, still in the location they were originally trucked to, were built in the 1980s or 90s, some even from the 70s, so these mobile homes have been in that location for a long time. They are not going anywhere, but they could be. They have a trailer hitch. They have wheels and, if necessary, can be moved.

Some terms can be confusing: modular home, manufactured home, mobile home and RV. All of these are manufactured in a factory. That being said, the terms manufactured homes and mobile homes usually mean the same thing. A modular home is more like a regular house in that it doesn't come with wheels and is placed on a foundation. It is built off site, pre-fabricated at the factory, transported in finished sections to the land where it will sit permanently on a foundation, and is assembled by the builder at that site. A mobile home has wheels on it and a trailer hitch. It is brought to its destination on a trailer. It doesn't need to be assembled, unless it is a double, triple, or quadruple wide mobile home, in which case the assembly of the home is minimal, compared to even a modular home. It is not placed in a foundation. It can be, but most of the time it's not. An RV, a recreational vehicle, can be anything from a camper that is towed behind your car, to a large RV that's basically a house on wheels that is driven around the country. It cannot be placed on a foundation, nor is it built to be a permanent house for someone to live in on land. RVs were the precursors to the modern mobile home. When one looks at the mobile homes of the 60s, one can see their similarities. Today's RVs are, however, not the mobile homes of today. RVs are something that can be lived in temporarily and driven. For the purpose of this book, a mobile home is a home manufactured at a factory, placed in its entirety on trailer(s), trucked to a mobile home park, where it is set on cinder blocks or piers to remain there for years. Its wheels and hitch are stowed under the home for potential future use. Once skirting is placed between the base of the home and the ground, and a deck or stairs are placed on the side, it looks almost like a nice, regular house.

So how many people and what age groups live in mobile homes? About 22 million Americans live in mobile homes. The average age of a person who lives in a mobile home is 54. That is not to say that most people who live in mobile homes are over 55. Many of those people living in mobile homes are families. Some are single. Some are older. Some are younger. There are lots of different reasons why people choose to live in a mobile home at all walks of life.

Why is a mobile home such a viable alternative to an apartment or a house? It is often less expensive than renting an apartment or house. Of the people I have secured mobile homes for, I have been able to save them $200, $300, even $400 a month compared to where they were previously renting. This is a very significant reason to buy and move into a mobile home.

Another advantage of purchasing a mobile home is that the end buyer is going to own this home free and clear in four to six years. How many people in regular houses get a 4 year mortgage? They get a 30 year mortgage, sometimes a 15 year mortgage, but a 4 year mortgage is unheard of. These mobile homes cost one tenth if not one twentieth of what people pay for a 3 bedroom / 2 bath regular house. Some mobile homes come with garages or carports, and sheds. Many come with laundry rooms, sunken tubs and skylights, which are perks seen in nice regular houses.

Another reason why mobile homes are a reasonable alternative to an apartment or a rented house is that the resident owns a piece of the American dream. This is her home; she owns it from day one. As the owner of this home, she will have something to sell when she moves, unlike renting an apartment or a house.

Banks are not lending the way they used to and most banks don't loan for mobile homes. There are some banks that do, but they don't want to loan under $20,000. Most banks won't loan under $50,000. Unlike a regular house, which theoretically appreciates with value, a mobile home, because it is literally considered a vehicle, depreciates year to year. Banks aren't keen on loaning on an asset that depreciates. Banks do provide auto loans and they depreciate. A mobile home is not a car... or is it? It has a title just like a car.

Banks are also not eager to loan money for mobile homes because the people who move into mobile homes generally do not have good credit scores. They are considered too risky by most banks. In a later chapter on buyers, I will discuss why it is that, although the banks may not want to risk loaning to these people, they can be a very reasonable risks for an investor. These are people who you will vet carefully to make sure that they will be able to pay their loans off.

Another reason that buying a mobile home is a viable alternative to renting an apartment or a house is that it may be easier for the individual to be approved by the park than by a bank. The park will generally look at income and sometimes the park will look at credit. But when a park does consider credit, credit scores are either not a deciding factor or don't have to be that high to qualify living in the community. Those parks that do have high qualifications are not usually the parks you will be looking to work with. Residents in these parks can usually get bank loans or pay cash.

You will not be looking at the double, triple or quadruple wide mobile homes. You will not be looking at mobile homes that are in expensive communities. You will be looking for homes in a mobile home park where you are able to purchase a mobile home for $10,000 or less and the average mobile home sells for under $20,000.

Some banks that finance mobile homes ask for a 40% down payment. If a person, who wanted to live in a mobile home, saw one for sale for $10,000, she would have to come up with a $4,000 down payment. If a person is paying $10,000 for the place that she is going to live in, is she generally going to have $4,000 in her pocket to be able to pay for the down payment on that $10,000 purchase? Probably not.

The program, discussed in this book, allows the person, who will be ultimately living in the mobile home, to finance her mobile home with no money down! This is a huge benefit because the potential owner often has the means to pay every month but does not have the down payment. Her low credit score and lack of down payment means she may not qualify with the banks or the third party lenders offered at some mobile home parks, which use a similar qualification process to banks. Sometimes it seems that if someone who wants to live in a mobile home does not have 100% in cash, she cannot buy a mobile home.

There is a movement throughout the country right now called the "Tiny House Movement." It is becoming popular to live in really small houses (100-400 square feet). There are already communities of tiny houses throughout the country. These homes are usually more expensive, and definitely smaller than the mobile homes that this book focuses on buying and selling. But on the wave of this movement comes the less extreme version of people who just want a smaller, simpler lifestyle. Mobile homes and mobile home communities fit this need.

So how can investing in mobile homes be more lucrative than regular Real Estate? Well, for the investor, it has the advantage of renting without the disadvantages of being a landlord. There are monthly checks in the mail month after month for at least four years. Since the person living in the mobile home owns it from the day she signs that bill of sale, she is responsible for any and all repairs to the premises. There are no plugged toilet calls at two a.m. There is no waiting six months until the fix and flip is completed before you get a check. Profits from the fix and flip are rarely as much as initially calculated due to a variety of reasons. Maybe the calculation of the cost of redoing all the electrical was not in the initial estimate or the delays from the city permits division causes the project to halt causing holding costs to rise. The initial investment in a mobile home is so much lower than renting or fixing and flipping. A down payment on a traditional purchase of a $100,000 house to be used as a rental is 20% of the purchase price ($20,000), plus closing costs ($5,000), plus getting a house ready to rent, barring any major repair needed ($15,000). A minimum of $40,000 is required in this scenario. For a fix and flip over $200,000 may be required for initial investment. Comparatively, $10,000 (usually the most I spend on a mobile home) is not a huge amount of money to invest. The annual yield is similar to fix and flips. It has the stability of monthly income like a four year Certificate of Deposit. Month after month after month, payments will come to you. If you implement this system correctly, you could double your money or more in 4 years and you will have the ability to provide decent affordable housing to a sometimes forgotten population, to a population of hard working Americans who make less than $50,000 a year.

Now in a nutshell, what is the system and how does the system work? Greater detail on this system will be shown in several other chapters, but in a nutshell, this is how the system works:

1) You find a qualified buyer (The person who will ultimately own and live in the mobile home).
2) You find a qualified mobile home for sale that this person likes and can afford.

3) You pay cash to purchase the mobile home.

4) You sell the mobile home with seller financing on terms to the qualified buyer.

   The ideal numbers in a mobile home deal are buying the mobile home for $5,000 and selling it for $10,000 at 18.5% for 4 years. No down payment would be required. This is a huge return on investment!

5) You receive a check in the mailbox month after month.

In what other investment can you more than double your initial investment in 4 years? That's well over 100% return on investment in 4 years, and that's if you use your own money.

$$ROI\ on\ monufactured\ home\ @\ 18.5\% = \frac{\$(296^* \times 48) - \$5,000}{\$5,000}$$

$$= \frac{\$14,208 - 5,000}{\$5,000} = \frac{\$9208}{\$5,000} = 1.84 = 184\%$$

Your return on investment is 184%.

*$296 is the amortized monthly payment of a $10,000 loan, calculated at 18.5% over 4 years.

If you use someone else's money, your ROI is even higher because you have invested none of your own money. In this next example, your investor loans you $5,000, with which you buy the mobile home. If you repay him 7% amortized over four years, your monthly payment to your investor would be $120/mo. Note that your revenue from your buyer is $296/mo., so your net income is $176/mo.

$$ROI \ on \ Manufactured \ home \ @ \ 18.5\% = \frac{\$(176 \ x \ 48) - \$0}{\$0}$$

$$= \frac{\$8448}{\$0} = an \ infinite \ ROI$$

If you are not gaging the interest charged to your buyer on having to pay your investor, you can charge whatever percentage rate you feel is appropriate, depending on the risk you are willing to take with the buyer and on what monthly payment he can afford. It could be 0%. It could be higher than 18%. There are limits as to how high you can charge. There is a certain point where too high an interest rate is considered gouging. The government has laws that protect the consumer in that case. You are here to help others without losing money, but you are not gouging your clients to make an unreasonable profit either. What matters to most of the people you'll be working with is, "How much per month is this going to cost me, and can I afford it?"

Using the system, as described briefly above, can allow you to increase your ROI , resulting in your receiving in a check in your mailbox, month after month after month. The systems that will allow you these returns will be discussed in great detail throughout the rest of the book.

To compare return on investments, let's take a look at one of my mobile home transactions.

1) I purchased a mobile home for $10, 000
2) I put a sign in the window which said:
   > For Sale
   > Owner Financing
   > 0% Interest
   > Phone Number
3) Less than 3 weeks later I had a buyer who wanted to purchase the mobile home for $21,000. I was able to set up monthly payments that worked for her.
4) I started to get checks in the mail – month after month after month.

Note in this transaction, I bought the home first and I wasn't charging any percent interest. I was still developing my system. In the next chapter I will discuss how finding the buyer first mitigates risk. When other people want to invest in you, investors will want to have a good return on their money. Since this was early on in my investing in mobile homes, I stated 0% interest on the sign because I was using only my own money. There was no need for me to charge more. Even without charging interest, I had over 100% return on my investment over the course of the investment. Not only was all of my initial investment returned to me, my additional gain was $11,000. Who gets over a 110% ROI in four years? That became a model for what I was going to do later. That was also the most expensive mobile home that I have purchased.

You may be thinking: "This is amazing, but I can't do that. I have no time. I have money sitting in a money market account, but it's not making this kind of return. There is no way." How can you solve this dilemma? You could find a real estate investor who specializes in mobile homes, who is willing to do the time consuming work, to cut you into the deal. As the investor in that person's project, you could be asking for a rate of return possibly between 8% and 12%. I usually use 10% as the standard rate of return when calculating my numbers for a given deal, but it varies from investor to investor. Whatever percent you both agree on, the investor will receive a steady check in the mail for the next four years.

VERY IMPORTANT: It is of the utmost importance to be sure that the person whom you are handing your money to is someone who knows what he is doing. Reading this book will give you a good idea as to what are the right questions to ask and knowing what answers you should expect from someone who knows what he is doing in this business. Before you just hand someone your money, make sure that you are well educated about the investment you are about to make.

Another possible way of getting into the manufactured home market is to be an equity partner. You and another investor would both invest time and money in a specific mobile home deal. You agree to split the investment in the deal and the rewards or risks of the deal. Maybe your partner will contribute 75% of the work and 25% of the money and since you have little time, but you have money, you agree to contribute 75% of the money and 25% of the work. Then the two of you decide in advance and in writing what percent of the risks and rewards you will each receive.

There is, theoretically, more risk in being an equity partner than a financial investor in a project. If you are an equity partner and something goes awry, you both share the risk, so you both lose money. Of course, if something goes well (and it should, if you follow this system), you will have a high reward. The reason I say that it is riskier is that, if you are a financial investor in a project, the other person is taking the risk. If something goes awry, that person should still owe you money if you set up the promissory note correctly. There are always risks in any investment, but if the person with the deal just takes your money, that is a crime. It is often hard to prove that it is a crime, so buyers beware. Know your investment and know the person you are dealing with. If you are a financial investor in a deal, one would hope you would have signed paperwork that protects you regardless of how the deal goes.

I recently invested money in an apartment complex that was being built. The deal folded. Instead of the developer saying "too bad, I lost your money," he offered me an alternate investment with less risk and a set percent return over the next few years. In spite of the developer's issues with the projects he was working on, he stood behind his word and gave me the opportunity to continue to earn a return with him. It was the right thing to do. It also branded this person as someone who stands behind his word. Because he stood behind his word, I am more likely to do business with him in the future. The key is to be educated about what you are doing. Learn the questions to ask and the answers you should receive. Being informed as to how a deal should work will reduce the risk of your money being stolen. It may also reduce the risk of something going wrong with a deal with your equity partner.

So your choices again are: if you have money but no time, you could invest your money in someone else's deal and he can do all the work, or you can be an equity partner, with you and another investor splitting the investment of time and money and risking the losses or gains depending on how the deal goes.

You may have lots of time, but no money. You know that you could make a good return, if you only had the money. How can you solve this problem? There are several ways in which you can purchase mobile homes, even if you have no money:

1) You could become educated in how to do mobile home deals by reading, taking classes or shadowing someone who is successful in doing mobile home deals. Then give someone the opportunity to invest in your deals. This is often difficult, though not impossible, without your having a successful track record! After a couple of deals under your belt, this is a good plan. The faster you can get away from spending your own money, the better.

2) Perhaps you own a regular house of your own. You could purchase a mobile home by using the money from a "cash out" option, when you refinance your own house. I have purchased mobile homes this way. Instead of just refinancing your personal house to reduce your monthly payment, leverage the equity in your house to acquire mobile homes. Talk to your mortgage broker or banker about this possibility. This option allows you to borrow from the equity in your house, to purchase a mobile home or invest in a mobile home, at a lower interest rate than other borrowing options, like a credit card. It can be done.

3) You can charge it. You can buy a mobile home with a credit card. You are probably thinking, "Charge it! Are you insane? Didn't you just say in the last paragraph that a credit card was a higher interest borrowing option? " Well, what would you have done at the beginning of the chapter when I talked about purchasing the television set? Would you not have charged it? It is very likely, you would have. So why can't you charge the mobile home to your

credit card, so long as you charge it on a credit card with zero percent or a low percentage rate? I am not suggesting you charge it to a credit card that you have almost maxed out or to a credit card that has a 33% interest rate. You can use those promotional blank checks that come with your credit card and charge it to your low interest credit card.

4) You could actually use your self-directed IRA to purchase this mobile home. I talked a little bit in the introduction about how one of the ideal ways to purchase a mobile home is with a self-directed Roth IRA, because you are not going to be paying taxes on the gains. Gains earned through investing in a self-directed Roth IRA are not taxable because you have already been taxed on the income before you invested it in the self-directed Roth IRA. If you're not using a self-directed Roth IRA, you will pay taxes on the gains from your mobile home investment in the year that you buy and sell this mobile home – not the year it is completely paid off, but the year you sell it to the end buyer. So if you pay cash, use a credit card, or pay for it with the equity in your personal house; that's the year that you are going to be paying your capital gains. So, buying a mobile home right off the bat within a Roth self-directed IRA is your best bet because those gains are not taxed.

5) You could borrow from a friend or relative. This is something I have done with mobile homes. Some have been equity partners where we split the investment of time and money between us and

also the gains. Some have been debt partners who receive an agreed upon APR over the length of the loan. You can agree on whatever terms you want with your friend or relative.

In all these scenarios, remember that you are usually paying for the mobile home with physical cash, not writing a check. To pay for the mobile home, you will need to cash that credit card check, take cash out of your IRA, cash the check received after your "cash out" when refinancing your regular house or cash the check from your friend or relative to pay for the mobile home. Cash is king in buying mobile homes.

On a side note, you could also buy the mobile home personally or with your LLC or corporation using cash you already have. This section is about buying a mobile home if you don't have the cash readily available.

Now by this point in the chapter, you know that you can make money in the manufactured home market. You also know there are many reasons ethically and financially why investing in the manufactured mobile home market is a great idea and will increase your ROI. But now what? How do you start? Should you start by finding a mobile home for under $10,000 and buying it? Oh no, no, no, no! I have done that (my very first deal) and I will explain in the next chapter why you do not want to start out the way I did. Right now, you have to first find a buyer, and that's what the next chapter is about, so quickly go to the next chapter and find out what you need to do to find a buyer.

2
THE BUYER WINS!
Who's In Need of a New Home?
The New Buyer!

How to Find the Buyer and the Right Mobile Home for the Buyer's New Beginning

You win (you profit) when you find those who are in need and you supply those needs. The more you see who is in need, the more needs are met. The more needs are met, the more you WIN or profit. In this chapter, we're going to take a look at the needs of the buyer and learn how to supply those needs.

A. Why Finding the Buyer First is Paramount

Why would you look for a buyer before you have something to sell? There are some very important reasons for that. Finding the buyer first is paramount! If I purchase a mobile home, what will happen if I don't find a buyer soon? Once, I got a really good deal on a mobile home, but I didn't have a buyer. Month after month I lost money. What drained my resources? The same thing that was draining the seller's resources - lot rent.

In the mobile home parks I work with, the park owns the land and the residents own the mobile homes. Each resident signs a lease on the land, committing him to pay lot rent each month for usually one year. It is renewed every year the mobile home is on the park's land. A resident could move it. It is a mobile home, right? That could cost $2,000-5,000 or more, depending on how far it is being moved. Moving the mobile home is more of an immediate financial burden than the monthly lot rent. Furthermore, where would it be moved to? Is the mobile home worth moving? So, if this resident were trying to sell his mobile home, he would continue to pay lot rent month after month. He may reduce his price in the hope that someone will buy it and end his monthly commitment to lot rent. The lease on the land is attached to the mobile home, so when the new homeowner moves in, this person will sign a new lease with the park and the seller is finally free of lot rent.

The average lot rent in the Chicagoland area ranges from $400-800 a month. I have seen lot rent as low as $170 and as high as $1,200. When I bought my first mobile home, it seemed like a really good deal, but I couldn't find a buyer, so I paid lot rent month after month. Did that money work for me? No! Month after month, my money went into the park's pocket. If I had an investor who paid for this mobile home, I would have had to start paying him back month after month from the day I bought the mobile home. Not a good situation. So it's very, very important that you have a buyer first. Here is an example of my biggest mistake.

I found a nice little one bedroom mobile home, about 800 square feet for $3,500 dollars. It seemed to be in a very neat, very clean mobile home park. There was not that much that really needed to be done to this mobile home. Some light fixtures needed to be changed, fresh paint was needed over the interior paneling, a new deck was built for the front door, and a few more things were done to update it. So I thought, "Wonderful. I'll put all these things in it and I'll improve the mobile home and then I will put it on the market."…. And no one responded. And I kept putting it on the market….Still no one responded. I got very creative in the ads…. Still no one responded. I put up flyers at grocery stores and restaurants… Still no one responded. I even slept in the mobile home and practically went door-to-door asking people to purchase this mobile home from me. I had open houses where I met many neighbors who came over for cookies and lemonade in the summer months and hot chocolate in the winter. It did make the year enjoyable. They were very nice neighbors, but it did not sell the mobile home. It was almost an entire year before I was able to sell the mobile home. By that time, I was ready to give it away. A couple who needed to move in immediately did buy it for $10,000, so I did meet their needs, and they have been very happy in the mobile home, but my journey was much longer and much more expensive than anticipated.

It was a nice mobile home. It was in a very nice mobile home park. In fact, the park was so meticulous that the lawn was to be kept exactly four inches high. The park owner, who mowed everyone's lawn, maintained the lawn at that height. Other aspects of the mobile home park were very well kept too. There were nice roads, with curbs and mailboxes in front of each mobile home. Garbage was collected twice a week. It was a beautiful little mobile home park, right on the edge of a forest preserve. The residents did enjoy the forest preserve. Many residents liked to bike and walk around the mobile home park and in the preserve. Because of the preserve, deer walked by the window of the mobile home. It was beautiful. I tried to emphasize the positive nature of the park in my ads, because in the park itself, I felt quite safe.

But to get to this Eden, any prospective buyers had to drive through boarded up buildings, and past an abandoned K-mart, with grass growing through the parking lot. And there were other problems that sabotaged the selling of this mobile home. This mobile home park was located in an area that did not support its growth with jobs. It was adjacent to an area where crime was rising. All around it were other mobile home parks, which were not doing much better. The mobile home was located in a 55 plus park, thus reducing the pool of potential buyers. The other mobile homes parks were all-ages parks.

I learned several important lessons that year about buying and selling mobile homes. First, I was grateful for the new friends I met in the park and realized the importance of relational capital in a mobile home community. I will go into more details in a later chapter as to what that term means, but basically it is nurturing relationships to benefit both parties. I frequently visited with my new friends whenever I was at the park. Some friends kept an eye on the mobile home I was selling when I wasn't there. Others told me what was happening with the park management, including how many mobile homes were actually empty. This park did not permit "For Sale" signs in the windows, either, making it difficult to sell the home and to see how empty the park actually was. One of the residents referred me to someone outside the park for a Real Estate deal. Secondly, I learned, I would be very careful about buying a mobile home with one bedroom again because the buyers' pool is too small. Thirdly, I learned to be very aware of the crime in the surrounding area near the mobile home park. Most importantly, I decided to always have a buyer before finding a mobile home for the buyer to live in.

B. Who is Your Buyer?

Who is the buyer? Your buyer typically makes $2,000-4,000 a month, which is an hourly rate of $12.50-25.00 in a 40 hour week. That comes to about $24,000-48,000 a year. Given that income, she could be on government stipends, she could be on disability or social security or it could be her wage. The people in this category are not poverty stricken. They are hard-working, or if they're on social security, they were hard-working, wage-earning Americans. According to the 2010 census, about 25% of all American households fall in this income category. This is a difficult financial place to be because it is just above what the government considers to be the poverty threshold for a family of four. Those making above $48,000 can more easily handle a major purchase such as a car or an unexpected medical bill. Those people making under $48,000 annually are often living paycheck to paycheck. Many are scraping by to meet their basic monthly expenses. Can you help these people get the American dream they did not think was possible? Can you get them into affordable housing in a decent neighborhood? Yes, you can!

What else do you know about the buyer? She could make a much higher wage than what I just described, but perhaps had made poor financial choices or experienced a hiccup in her finances. Possibly, she may even have been devastated by the last recession.

Many of the people who are going to be your buyers have no savings. The buyer usually cannot afford a down payment, but can afford monthly payments. These are hard-working people who make $24,000-48,000 a year. They often have no credit or poor credit. Sometimes the potential buyer might actually have good credit, but does not qualify with the bank. There was a situation I knew of where a couple was applying for loan at a bank for a mobile home that they felt that they could afford. They had the income and even had the down payment. But there was something wrong. They had paid one credit card off, thinking it would give them better credit. The bank didn't see it that way. Apparently, they picked the wrong card. The loan was refused. The Park office told them about me and the couple called me.

More likely, the buyer will have low to no credit. Occasionally, you may get someone with very good credit, but not enough down payment to satisfy the bank or some other issue or problem that the bank sees, like in the case above. Your buyer will need to show you proof of income, so that you will be able to rely on him to pay you back on the note month after month.

If you are going to follow this system unaided, you'll have to make sure that the person who you are loaning this money to, is going to pay you your money back. If an investor is investing in your business, you have to make sure that you can assure the investor, that the potential buyer, she is loaning this money to, is someone the investor can count on, and you can count on, or you may still owe the investor money, even if the buyer doesn't pay you.

There is a price for the American dream, but in a mobile home park, this dream is reachable to many more people through you. To help a person succeed at acquiring his American dream, you need to make sure that the person who wants to buy the mobile home has an income of at least three times the lot rent, preferably three times the lot rent plus what his monthly house payment will be. You need to make sure that your buyer knows what his specific needs are in a home, financially, geographically, physically, and you need to know how fast he needs to move in. Possibly, he would need some encouragement to provide information in these areas. Using the application, found later in this chapter, will allow you to quickly assess his needs.

Talking with the potential buyer and beginning to create relational capital with the buyer, from the first time you meet him, is very important. Creating relational capital with this buyer, may encourage him to tell his friends about you. The way you develop your relationship with him could lead to not just a successful deal with him, but the very deal that his friend wants to make later. Who knows who that friend will refer you to? So, it's important to always realize that relational capital is vital even in the early stages of this process.

Usually, your buyer is going to be looking for a 2-3 bedroom mobile home with minimal required repairs. It is less usual that a potential buyer is looking for a one bedroom mobile home, but it is possible.

Is your potential buyer going to take pride in home ownership? Will he be an asset to the park? If he has pride in home ownership, he is more likely to be responsible in paying back your note and taking care of the home. In your conversations with the potential buyer, he may talk of planting a garden or mowing the grass. You can tell whether this person is someone who is going to take pride in home ownership when you start showing him the first mobile home and he says: "My couch can go over here", or "I think I'll put mini-blinds there". As you listen to your buyer--and this is a vital point--you will not only learn what his needs are, you will learn what kind of quality borrower he is going to be. You will see if you can take a risk on creating a note that allows him to own his own home. You will also have a good idea if this is a person who is willing to follow the rules of the mobile home park that he may be living in. Does he sound respectful of you and the park? If not, move on.

Your buyer is a hard-working American who deserves to have a place to live. Your buyers could be all ages, consisting of singles, couples, and families. About half of the people who live in mobile home parks are over the age of 55.

So, who is *not* your buyer? Your buyer is usually not someone who can pay cash, or someone who can get a bank loan. Your buyer is not a criminal. The mobile home park that he will live in will probably do a criminal background check. If your buyer does not pass the criminal background check, the park generally will not rent the land to him. It is good that the park has done this background check because if he does not pass, he is not someone we're going to be able to rely on to pay back the note month after month. Check any adult who will be living in the mobile home too. The other day I was about to show a mobile home to a potential buyer, who came well recommended and had the income to qualify, but right before the appointment, he confessed." My wife is in prison for a serious drug offense and so the park will reject us". He was absolutely right. If he had been caught living in a mobile home with this type of criminal background, he would have been evicted. You do all you can to set your clients up to win.

Another person, who is not your buyer, is someone who can't get over the stigma of her residence being a mobile home. And that's too bad, because so many people in America could benefit from living in mobile homes. With 25% of the population earning $24,000-48,000 a year, there's a huge segment of the population that you could be helping. Currently, 22.5 million people already live in mobile home parks, but there are so many more that could take advantage of mobile homes as a possible residence.

Another person you don't want as a potential buyer is someone who wastes your time. If she changes her mind about what she wants over and over, and ends up looking at lots and lots of mobile homes, this is a waste of your time and it is a waste of her time. This is why qualifying the buyer and finding out exactly what she needs before you show her that first mobile home is so important.

C. Why is living in a Mobile Home a Viable Alternative to Living in an Apartment or House?

Before you talk to any potential buyers, before you qualify anyone, you need to understand why living in a mobile home is such a viable alternative to living in an apartment or renting or even buying a house, so that when you talk to a potential buyer, you will understand why a mobile home is a residence she definitely will want to call home.

The monthly housing cost of living in a mobile home is usually less expensive than renting an apartment. In a mobile home park, there are two payments for housing. One is lot rent, and the other is a loan payment for the mobile home, if the owner borrows money to buy the mobile home. So, the person who moves into the mobile home pays to rent the land, and also pays for the mobile home. I have found that, even with lot rent and a house payment, the cost of living in a mobile home is significantly less than renting a house or apartment. The clients I've worked with have saved $200, $300, even $400 a month compared to the cost of their previous housing situation, usually renting an apartment or house. That savings includes the lot rent and the payment to me. Once the buyer is no longer paying installments on the mobile home, her monthly housing cost will be reduced to just lot rent, saving her even more.

Another important reason that mobile homes are a viable alternative to an apartment or house is that the resident of a mobile home is not sharing a wall. This is the buyer's mobile home. This is the buyer's separate unit. He doesn't have to deal with neighbors with an adjoining wall.

The buyer will probably own the mobile home free and clear in four years. How many four year mortgages are out there for a regular house? None that I know of. These are decent 2 bedroom mobile homes from 700 to 1100 square feet in size. You are not renting the mobile home to the buyer. You don't own the land. Under most circumstances, you can't rent. Nor will you want to. Renters generally don't take care of a home the way home owners do.

This is the buyer's home from day one. The buyer owns it. She is responsible for it. She can own the American dream. I had a woman who said to me, "I never thought I could own my own house. I never thought this was even possible. I thought all I could do for the rest of my life was rent." She was so excited to actually be able to own her home and to own it free and clear in four years. She is so grateful.

Using this mobile home program, the buyer can move in fast. In my last two deals, a new owner moved into the mobile home less than a week after the initial contact with me. There is not a 30-40 day delay in the purchasing of a mobile home, as is often the case in a regular house It's important, that once you have all your ducks in a row, when you have your buyer, seller, mobile home, and paperwork, and you're ready to go that you get those papers into the hands of the new buyer and you get it closed as fast as you can, so you can start receiving those payments month after month after month.

A huge advantage to living in a mobile home is that, unlike renting, the person living in the mobile home has something to sell when he moves. With good relational capital, the person you sold the mobile home to could be the person who sells it back to you when he is ready to move out.

When mobile home owners work with me, if the homeowner communicates to me that his financial situation has changed in some way, I can also adjust the note payments to make the mobile home more affordable for the end buyer. I stretched a note to six years that had been four years to make it more affordable for the buyer and she has never missed a payment. Who does that with rent? No one that I know of.

It is not hard to qualify to live in a mobile home park. Credit does not have to be high to qualify; if the park requires that high of a credit score, it is probably not a park that you will want to work with. I will get into more detail on that in the mobile home parks chapter. Banks, though, want higher credit scores. This mobile home program does what banks can't; it allows some people, whom the banks have rejected, to be homeowners. Banks are not loaning like they used to. Although there are some banks that loan money for the purchase of a mobile home, there are very, very few lending institutions loaning for mobile homes that are priced under $20,000. This is a niche market where you can really meet a need.

The mobile home park takes care of outside amenities. This could include maintenance of roads, common areas, sanitation, water and waste systems, getting electricity to the mobile homes, providing gas or propane for the mobile homes, maintenance of common areas, and possibly even a pool or clubhouse. Some may even have resort amenities. Many of the burdens of home ownership are eliminated.

Each mobile home park has its own unique atmosphere. The tight knit, warm community is a huge advantage in a mobile home park. The buyer can choose the atmosphere of the neighborhood he wants to live in. The atmosphere of the park is often noticed by the buyer when he first visits a mobile home in the park. He will be able to tell if this is a place he wants to live in. I had one buyer who said to me, "I could die here. I love it." Listening to your buyer is very important. The community your buyer is about to live in is often a very tight knit community. The buyer is not sharing a wall, like in an apartment and sometimes there is even a little yard, car port, or even a garage or shed. There are spaces between mobile homes in a mobile home park but, generally, the resident of a mobile home is still not very far from his neighbor. When I was trying to sell that mobile home that just wouldn't sell, I spent a lot of time in the mobile home. I got to know the neighbors well. I still keep in touch with some of those neighbors, even though some have moved to other places. A mobile home park can be a very friendly atmosphere to live in.

Some buyers are turning to mobile homes as a more sustainable and environmentally friendly lifestyle. Smaller homes use less energy and less space.

D. Finding the Buyer

How do you find the buyer? There are several different ways in which you can advertise to try to find a buyer. On the internet, there are three places that I have found helpful for advertising mobile homes. One is Craigslist. Specifically advertise under "manufactured homes" when advertising on Craigslist. Two sites that specialize in mobile home sales are MH village and MH Bay. I've used the latter two to look for mobile homes that are for sale, but I've generally used Craigslist to advertise mobile homes that I am selling. I have found it also helpful to create fliers that I can put up, especially the ones that have the tags on the bottom that can be torn off. The fliers can be put up in local grocery stores, restaurants, hardware stores, community centers, gas stations, college kiosks and other places that will allow me to put up fliers. Checking with a manager at many different types of places is key.

As far as using paid advertisements, I suggest penny savers, free magazines that someone might pick up at the grocery store. One of the ones I have used in the Chicagoland area is called the Orange Peel Gazette. It is very reasonably priced and the ad runs for 3 months. I've had just the right amount of returns from it, and found it to be very helpful. What's really amazing is that not all the buyers for mobile homes will actually have a computer, or access to one. Reaching them may be tricky in today's marketing world, where so much marketing is done online. That's where a less techie approach is more likely to reach these buyers, such as posting flyers or advertising in the local newspaper. You might even be able to post an ad in the mobile home park office. In advertising for a buyer, one thing you could emphasize is the comfort of home, and the safety of a mobile home community. Mobile home communities are tight and that's what often makes them safe. They basically have their own neighborhood watch going on all the time. In the chapter on mobile home parks, you will see red flags for communities you will not want to purchase mobile homes in.

Be careful of the way you advertise. You are not a lending institution, nor should you pose as one. You are not a Realtor, nor should you pose as one.

This is what my typical ad says:

Mobile Home for Sale
No Banks
No Down payment required
Flexible Terms
Call: xxx-xxx-xxxx

Because mobile home communities are so tight, word gets around fast. If you help someone buy a mobile home, the new buyer may think what you did to facilitate his living in a mobile home is amazing. He will talk to friends and neighbors who also might want you to help them find a mobile home too. I can't tell you how many people I've talked to who have said, "I've never heard of this. I didn't know this was even possible."

Another way to receive leads is from a park that you've worked with before. Park management may call to let you know, "Someone called our park today, but did not qualify for the loan. Can you help her?" Receiving leads is a very good reason to establish a good relationship with park management.

Maybe Realtors who you have worked with could refer buyers to you. A person may have come to the Realtor to rent or buy a regular house. He may have tried to qualify for a house, but was turned down. The Realtor might remember you and pass these leads on to you because a mobile home may be a better fit. You may help the Realtor in some other circumstance.

There are a few Realtors who specialize in mobile homes. A Realtor may have a mobile home for sale, but if a buyer interested in the mobile home she has for sale does not qualify for a bank loan, the Realtor can contact you. Once contacted, if you feel the buyer qualifies for your mobile home program, you'll be able to get the Realtor her commission check a little faster.

Another way to get leads is from other investors. I've had other investors call me and say, "I've got this lead; it doesn't work for me. Perhaps it will work for you." Again, if I find something that I can help them with, I will. A couple of online investor sites that I've found helpful have been REI Blackbook and REI Matcher. These websites help investors find other investors.

You could also check your local REIA (Real Estate Investors Association) or you could look for a Cash Flow Game night. These organizations can be found on Meetup.com. There are lots of networking opportunities with these organizations. You can find me on Meetup.com running a Cash Flow game night at least once a month in Aurora, IL. Cash Flow is a game designed by Robert Kiyosaki, author of *Rich Dad, Poor Dad* to teach people the basics of the accounting behind Real Estate deals. The game allows the player to simulate Real Estate transactions he might try in real life and develops the mindset for investing.

E. Qualifying the Buyer

How can you qualify the buyer? Here's an example of an application that I use when I'm qualifying buyers for mobile homes.

Applicant		Co- Applicant	
Name:		Name:	
Current Address:		Current Address:	
City		City	
State/Zip		State/Zip	
From:	To:	From:	To:
Cell Phone:	Home Phone:	Cell Phone:	Home Phone:
Email Address:		Email Address:	
What is the Best Way to Contact you?		What is the Best Way to Contact You?	
If residing less than 2 years at current address, Please provide your previous address and reason for move, on the back of this application		If residing less than 2 years at current address, Please provide your previous address and reason for move on the back of this application	
Income		**Income**	
Gross Monthly Income:		Gross Monthly Income:	
Current Employer:		Current Employer:	
Employer Contact Information:		Employer Contact Information:	
Other Source of Income:		Other Source of Income:	
Way to Verify Other Source of Income:		Way to Verify Other Source of Income:	
Your Mobile Home Requirements			
# of Bedrooms	# of Bathrooms		Square Feet
Desired Location			
What is your monthly housing budget excluding utilities?			
How much do you want to put down?			
When do you plan on moving?			
Pets?	How many pets?		What type of pets?
Would you prefer to live in a 55 + community?		Or would you prefer to live in an all Ages community?	
What amenities are you looking for in a park?			
References			
Name/Relation to you:	Email:		Phone:
1.			
2.			
I verify that the below information is correct.			
Signature of Applicant		Date:	
Signature of Co-Applicant		Date:	

Putting a letterhead at the top of the application makes it look even more professional. It's important that you make yourself look as professional as possible throughout this entire process. When I first made this application, I just had the word "Applicant" but now I have "Co-applicant" as well. It could be a husband or wife, or it could be a person who is co-signing for the applicant to live there. If a husband and wife apply, their combined incomes may qualify them. If for example, the applicant is an older person on social security who doesn't quite qualify, with say a son who has a full-time job, he may be a co-applicant although he's not living there. In this situation he would be co-signing on the loan for the mobile home and also co-signing on the lot rent. It is good to have that information for you and the park management, so that in case the mobile home payment or lot rent has not been paid, you can contact the co-applicant. The co-applicant is a backup needed in borderline cases. You should not solely depend on the co-applicant's income to qualify the buyer.

On the application, I ask: "What is the best way to contact you?" Some people really like to be contacted by phone, others would rather be contacted by email, and some would rather be texted or messaged through Facebook. Some people only communicate the way he or she prefers.

The reason I asked the question: "If residing less than 2 years at the current address, please provide your previous address and reason for move on the back of the application" is because I need to see a 4-year commitment from this person at this residence. I need to know that she is not going to move away in 6 months or a year, and that she has a steady income. If she lives somewhere 2 years or more, it sends a message of stability to me.

Besides asking the applicant to complete the above form, I may ask to see a copy of her latest pay stubs to verify her income, if I have permission to do so from her. I ask for the phone number of the employer on the application. The employer may not tell me necessarily how much the applicant is making, but will usually tell me whether the potential buyer is working there or not. I also ask for references. These are not necessarily references that will tell me how much she made or if she can afford to live there, but the references will tell me a little bit about the character of the potential buyer and if she is a person I can trust. It is important to trust the people that you work with. I trust that what the applicant writes down is correct, but I verify it, cementing a foundation of trust.

It's a short application, but it's very effective. I do not ask for a driver's license. I do not ask for a social security card. This is something the park will take care of. I am not a bank and I am not renting. The most important piece of information on this application, besides his name, is his gross monthly income. His gross monthly income divided by three should be able to cover the lot rent and his loan payment to you, but at the very least, the lot rent that is expected from the park.

You can't help everyone. People, who make less than $20,000 a year, are not as likely to receive your help. With that being said, I have taken applicants who make as little as $15,000. The numbers worked for her and she always paid on time. Once, a potential buyer contacted me and stated that she made only $250 a month. I could not help her. Government agencies may be available to help her, but that's not something I can help with. It's just not in the scope of what I am able to do. It's hard to turn people down, but I will not set someone up to fail. I want my buyer to be financially comfortable throughout the duration of the loan term. The person has to have a verifiable paycheck or other income. It could be a government check. It could even be from a temporary job. The applicant's income must be close to a one to three, housing to income ratio.

I do not perform credit or criminal background checks because the park generally does these. The credit check is usually a waste of time and money because most of the people who apply have low credit or no credit. I will ask verbally if the person or anyone who will be living in the household has been involved in any criminal activity that might show up when park management does its check. If that possibility exists, and the applicant lets me know, then I will talk directly to the park about the applicant's specific situation. There is no point wasting the park manager's time submitting a criminal check, or the applicant's money on an application fee for the criminal check, if the park management can tell you in advance that the individual's situation dictates she will likely be rejected.

F. Fulfilling Your Buyers Needs

Which mobile home will be the best fit for your buyer? You need to ask your buyer to prioritize his needs. Where does he want to live? What is important to him about where he wants to live? Is it the school district? Does he need to be near a hospital? Does he need to be near recreational facilities or public transportation? Listen carefully to your buyer. Sometimes, what he is not saying is more important than what he is saying. He may say, "I want to live in Springfield." Ask your buyer, what it is that he likes about Springfield. Is it because of the proximity to where his children will want to go to school or did he choose that location because he needed public transportation to get to work? Listen carefully to what your buyer is asking for, so you can best meet his needs and you waste less of your own time.

How much does your buyer want to pay every month? You know how much she makes according to what she has put on the application and you will verify it, but maybe she doesn't want to pay one third of her gross monthly income. Maybe she wants to pay an even smaller percentage of her monthly income for her housing. How fast does she need to move in? Are mobile homes available in the area? I had someone call the other day who wanted to move to a mobile home in a specific town in a specific area. I checked every mobile home park in that area. There was not a mobile home available at that time, and that happens sometimes. So, keep a person on your buyer's list even if you can't initially help her. She may still want a mobile home when one becomes available.

What size of a mobile home does your buyer need? Most of the mobile homes you offer will be 2 to 3 bedroom homes, usually 700 to 1,100 square feet in size. How new of a mobile home does your buyer want? Most of the mobile homes you will want to deal with are from the 1980s or newer. Maybe the applicant says he doesn't mind doing a little bit of repair on a mobile home that might need some TLC (Tender Loving Care). It is best to have the work done professionally. This benefits the potential new buyer in the end, because if the new buyer who says he is a handyman does not complete his work to code, and he wishes to sell the mobile home later, he may devalue the mobile home. You will want to try to look ahead to see what will benefit your client in the long run. For this reason, it is a good idea to only look for mobile homes that don't need a lot of repair, preferably less than 20% of the price the buyer will pay for the mobile home itself. It is also important for you to take care of the repairs, not just because you will demand a quality product, because it speeds up the implementation of the sales of the mobile home.

During one mobile home transaction, I had a qualified buyer; we agreed on a price. The park asked that I not purchase the mobile home until I agreed to paint the outside. I agreed to do so. It was a late 70s mobile home with metal siding; metal paint is expensive. I asked the park if there had been an estimate for how much it would cost to paint the outside of the mobile home. The manager informed me there had been an estimate for $2,000. I told the buyer of the situation and added the estimated cost of the repair into the loan for my new buyer. She did not blink an eye because it did not change her monthly payments (just added 8 months). Then I shopped around for someone who could paint a mobile home with metal paint. I was able to negotiate a price $500 lower than the park's estimate. I informed my new buyer that I was chopping two payments off the end of her loan. Now I look like I am the hero because I reduced how much I was charging her for the mobile home. This arrangement allowed her to get into a mobile home that she did not think was possible in only a few days. Wins all around!

A feature that your buyer should be looking for in a mobile home is air conditioning. In any part of this country, it's going to get hot in the summer. Mobile homes are going to heat up pretty fast because they do not have the same type of insulation as a regular house. Air conditioning is absolutely important. If there is a mobile home you're looking at that does not have central air conditioning, go and buy a couple of window air conditioners to stick in the windows. Just make sure there is the option of air conditioning in the mobile home. Sometimes one window air conditioner is enough to cool the whole home and they are fairly inexpensive.

Ceiling fans provide good air circulation on those warm summer nights so the air conditioner doesn't need to run all the time. Mobile homes should have operable windows throughout the home, creating nice cross ventilation. Although not absolutely necessary, having ceiling fans in the living room and bedrooms is a very nice perk that many clients will appreciate or be looking for.

Many mobile homes come with sheds or car ports or even a yard. Some even come with skylights, a fireplace or a sunken tub. Are any of these features ones that your buyer really wants in his home?

One thing to consider when you're speaking with your buyer is whether or not he wants to live in an age-restricted park. Does he want to live in a 55 plus park? Does he want to live in a family park? Does he have a dog? If so, what size is the dog? How much does the dog weigh? Is the dog considered an aggressive breed, such as a Pit Bull or Rottweiler? Some parks don't allow dogs at all. Some parks only allow small dogs. Some parks do not allow pets at all. One park I worked with said they allow one pet. The policy was that it could be a dog or a cat but would only allow one. It is important to make sure that the pet policies of the park match your buyer before you start looking at a mobile home for your buyer in that park.

At this price point for mobile homes, it's unusual that the park will have a lot of amenities such as a resort community, but, occasionally you can find these things. And these are extra perks you can show to your buyer that may help him decide between two mobile homes that are available. Besides swimming pools, some mobile home parks may have basketball courts, laundry rooms, or playgrounds. Some parks might even have golf courses or lakes inside their parks where the residents can fish or swim or boat. For the most part, mobile homes in this price range will not be in parks that have a lot of amenities. Make sure your buyer can actually afford what he wants and that it's available where he wants to live. If what he wants is not feasible, ask your buyer if he can reprioritize his needs and wants.

G. Buyer Miscellaneous

Do not qualify your buyer on potential future income. If he says to you, "My uncle Joe is going to hire me to work for him next week and I should be getting $25 an hour." You cannot base your decision to buy him a mobile home on what has not happened yet. You have to base your decision on his current situation. Telling a buyer that he can afford something that he does not yet have the income for, sets him up to fail at the outset. It is not a good business practice to do this. It is not good for the buyer, it tells your investors that your clients are not screened. Your investors could lose trust in you, or if the buyer can't pay, you ultimately lose money. Don't set your clients up to fail.

Make sure that you are taking control of the buying process. Know your bottom line. Don't waste too much time with a potential buyer. Know the end before you get started. Know where you need to end up financially before you even talk to your buyer. Know what your time is worth and make that clear to the buyer, so that he is not wasting your time. Make sure you are the one setting up the appointments to find the perfect mobile home. You will look at the mobile homes in advance, you will narrow it down to three mobile homes, and you will show the buyer one. If the buyer likes the first mobile home, there is no need to show the buyer any more. Once the buyer has chosen a mobile home, get the buyer approved at that park. There is no need to get the buyer approved at every park he's looking at a mobile home in, because it is a waste of his money to apply at every park.

It is your job to negotiate, not your buyer's job. You already know what your buyer can afford. It's your job to go to the seller and get a price so that you can make money and your buyer is happy with the size of the monthly payments. You can negotiate this so the seller is happy too!

Contact your investor to get his funds ready; then set up two closings. First, there is a closing where you buy the mobile home from the seller, and then a closing occurs where you sell the mobile home to the end buyer (the person who will be living in the mobile home). There is more information on closings and how those work in a later chapter. Finding the just right buyer is so important, or the rest of this process will not work.

Now that you have a buyer and your investor is on alert, that a mobile home may be purchased soon, it's time to identify the seller and the perfect mobile home for your buyer. How do you find someone selling the mobile home your buyer is looking for? That is what will be examined in the next chapter.

#3
THE SELLER WINS!
Who's In Need of Getting Rid of Property?
The Seller!

How to Identify and Help Distressed Sellers

The theme that weaves through this book is that, when you find out Who's In Need, and meet that need, you both WIN. In this chapter, the person who is in need is the seller. When you fulfill his need, you win, meaning you profit. And the seller wins too, because he receives what he needs. Previous chapters have covered what you are in need of, what the buyer is in need of, and now it is time to find the mobile home, and what the seller is in need of. So how can you find this distressed seller who wants to sell her mobile home?

A seller in a mobile home park is very distressed when she wants to sell. Why? An Owner of a mobile home is obligated to pay the rent on the land on which her home is located - even if the mobile home is paid off. Many mobile home parks have the home owners sign a one-year lease for the land. The lot rent on average is $400 - 700 a month, although I have seen lot rent as high as $1,200/ month. That is $14,400 a year, not for the mobile home, just for the land. Most Americans that live in mobile home parks do so because mobile homes are one of the most affordable housing options available. And it all works well, until there is a hiccup or a glitch. There are many reasons, which I will talk about later, as to why a person may need to move. When she does need to move, she must move immediately.... but the lot rent is killing her financially as month after month she is not able to sell her home. The mobile home owner is trapped. What will she do? The park is not motivated to help her sell. The mobile home owner has a lease and knows she is legally obligated to pay for the rest of the year.

She should call a Realtor – right? Most mobile homes are not sold through Realtors for two reasons. Mobile homes are not technically real estate. Furthermore, the average Realtor receives about a 6% commission. How much is that on a $7,000 mobile home? $420. Representing a mobile home is not really in the Realtor's best interest; it is not worth the Realtor's time at all. So, the owner puts a sign in her window and usually asks for an inflated price because she "knows" she has the best home in the park. She hopes for the best and no one bites. As time goes on, and her finances become more desperate, the mobile home falls into disrepair. The seller wants cash to pay for the hiccup in her life, but the potential buyers, who do look at the mobile home, don't have $7,000 in cash in their pockets. No one will loan to these buyers and the "for sale by owner" sign becomes faded with discouragement. This owner will do anything to get out of her situation. That is when the owner becomes a distressed seller and you may be able to help her.

Where can you find mobile homes for sale? There are some online sources that I use regularly, which I have mentioned before: Craigslist, MH Village and MH Bay. Zillow sometimes has mobile homes. Of those websites, the one I use most often is Craigslist. I get a good idea when looking at a Craigslist ad as to where the seller is coming from. The verbiage used tells me whether this is being sold by the park, the individual, or a person who desperately needs to get rid of this mobile home. It also shows me pictures of the condition of the mobile home. Take into consideration when looking at the pictures on Craigslist that sometimes you are only shown what the seller wants you to see.

Besides looking on the internet, just googling "Mobile homes for sale" in a particular town, and checking out the websites above, one of the most common ways to find out if a mobile home is for sale is to drive through local mobile home parks. Now you may wonder why it is that most of the mobile homes for sale are found just by driving through the park. Many sellers just place a sign in their window that says "Mobile Home for Sale." Many sellers don't necessarily advertise on the internet, in a newspaper, or anywhere else. The seller may or may not even put up fliers at the local grocery store. He may just take a sign, put it in his window, and hope for the best. Since many sales take place via word-of-mouth, when the seller puts a sign in his window, he assumes one of his neighbors will see it, or someone visiting his neighbors will see it, and will want to buy the mobile home. These are the signs you are trying to spot. These sellers are prime candidates for this program.

You may ask, wouldn't it just be easier to get on the computer, look up the mobile home park on their website and find out when the mobile homes are for sale? Oh, ho, it would be great if it were that easy. Many mobile home parks do not have websites. Those that do, have websites that only post the mobile homes that the park owns, not the "for sale by owner" mobile homes. Driving through parks seems to be the most effective way of finding mobile homes for sale.

Some parks don't allow "for sale" signs, which makes it difficult to sell in that neighborhood, or to find out what's for sale. The park could be half empty, and you wouldn't know it, because there would be no signs in any of the windows. This is a red flag you will look for, when you are finding parks you may not want to be working with. Besides driving through the parks, you can also find mobile home for sale ads in online newspapers, local newspapers, grocery stores or coffee house bulletin boards, or any place you see fliers posted.

The question is why wouldn't you normally work with a Realtor? You could call a Realtor and ask him if he has any mobile homes for sale. Most Realtors are not interested in selling a mobile home; it is just not worth him time for a couple hundred dollars to drive you around looking at mobile homes for sale. There was a particular Realtor I worked with, who took a $2,000 cut from the sale of each sold mobile home that he had listed, rather than a percent. If you can find a Realtor that specializes in mobile homes, and you can work with him, that would be wonderful. But if a Realtor is asking for a $2,000 cut, you have to ask yourself: how much does the seller want? How much is he going to raise his price in order to give the Realtor that cut? So a Realtor is not always your best bet. You just have to gage each situation.

As you find mobile homes for sale, how can you tell if the seller is a distressed seller? As you are looking through ads for mobile homes, notice the tone the writer uses describing his mobile home or himself. Oftentimes, you can see how distressed he is just by the words that he chooses in order to sell his mobile home. Look at the price. There are two things that you might notice: one, that the price is extremely cheap or extremely expensive. The reason those are the two extremes you want to take note of is that this may be an indication that the seller really wants to get out of the mobile home. Some people are willing to basically give away their mobile homes in order to avoid paying that lot rent month after month. The reason you may find a mobile home that is priced really high is that the seller may have a lot of bills to pay and other things he wants to spend that money on; he is counting on the sale of the mobile home to pay for those things. Maybe there is some way you know of for him to get the things he needs outside of selling his mobile home. He may then be willing to sell the mobile home to you at a discount. Of course, just like with regular houses, there is always the person who prices his home very high because he feels that his mobile home is the best one in the neighborhood. Read the ads, taking note of the kinds of circumstances listed in the ad and why he is selling his home. When you begin to speak with a distressed seller, spend a lot of time listening to him. Sometimes it's not what the seller is saying; it's what he is not saying where you can hear the circumstance as to why the person is selling his mobile home. How long has the mobile home been on the market? How old is that sign that you saw in the window? These are clues that you can use to identify a distressed seller.

Now, you won't work with just any distressed seller in just any mobile home. Remember, you are providing decent, affordable housing, so the mobile must be decent. Neither the house nor the neighborhood should be rundown.

The seller must have the title to the mobile home. There have been circumstances where the seller has said to me, "I can't find the title. I think I lost it years ago." I would not buy a mobile home if a person said that and refused to produce a title. But, if he is willing to go to the Department of Motor Vehicles (DMV) to reapply for a new title, then I would definitely consider working with him and I have. I must know that he was in the process of getting a new title before I can move forward with the offer. Communication is key every step of the way. If the seller cannot find the title, and he cannot produce the title, you cannot accept the keys to the mobile home or give him cash. Without that title, you cannot do business with him. The title must be a clean title. It cannot be one where money is owed on it. It's just one less thing that you have to deal with. You want to have a fast closing. Not having to deal with other liens expedites the process.

The price range of a mobile home you may consider could be listed as high as $20,000. Remember, you could buy a mobile home for up to $10,000, but no more than $10,000. You can always negotiate for a lower price. Once you start negotiating, it becomes a habit. Eventually, when finding a mobile home priced higher than you want to pay, you will no longer feel uncomfortable offering below what works for you. Negotiating will be discussed a bit more in a later chapter.

There are some repairs you will want to consider when choosing the right mobile home for your buyer, too. Make sure all the basics are working. As you walk through the mobile home, see if it's level. See if the heating and air conditioning are working. See if the water runs in all the faucets and see if it runs fully or weakly. If it is located in the northern area of the country, ask about the heat tape underneath the mobile home. Heat tape will be discussed more in the repair section. It is very important that mobile homes that have to survive northern winters have working heat tape on the pipes under the mobile home. Cosmetic repairs are usually not a problem; a person can move in with cosmetic repairs, but the mobile home must be livable. If the mobile home is in need of repair, it should not cost more than 20% of the price that the buyer will be paying you for the mobile home. You don't need that price going any higher; assume your investor is going to pay for this mobile home. The price of the mobile home must remain within the financial parameters set by you and your investor. If the offer increases to include repairs, you still don't want to be paying more than a total of $10,000 for this deal. If something needs to be done in order for the buyer to live in the mobile home, you add that to the buyer's costs. Make sure the buyer can still afford it.

The biggest red flag you want to look for in a mobile home is water damage. Check for water damage under windows and sinks. If the floor seems a little soft in spots, especially in the bathroom or under windows, in front of toilets, showers and tubs, or there are water spots and sagging areas on the ceiling, these indicators are big red flags. Most of the walls and floors in a mobile home are made of particle board, which absorbs water quickly. It gets soft, it holds moisture, it molds, it rots and it falls apart. I have seen toilets and tubs collapsed into the floors of mobile homes. A small sign of water damage might be a sign of a much larger and expensive problem. It can be a big deal. I have seen walls of mobile homes covered in white crystal mold. No, I did not buy those mobile homes. I ran.

Has the mobile home been on the market for a long while? These mobile homes are the ones you are looking for: the ones that have been on the market for a long time. It is hard to determine how long a mobile home has been on the market because there is no Zillow or Trulia for mobile homes that states the "days on market." This is where developing a relationship with the park management, or people living in the park, is helpful. If you have developed a good relationship, the park management will call you when there is a distressed seller. You can find a way to reward the park manager: with leads for the park or a finder's fee or a gift certificate to a local restaurant or attraction.

Maybe the manager is happy just finding a buyer for that mobile home. But if you do something special, that $20 gift certificate may earn you thousands of dollars in the future. As you get to know people, you will find what motivates each person to help you.

The owner of the mobile home may have died or may be going to a nursing home. The heirs of the owner may want to get rid of the mobile home, but the heirs may have more pressing matters to deal with other than selling a mobile home. Maybe a parent is being placed in a senior care facility. The adult-children of the owner may want to be with their parent, spending time with her. If the heirs don't want to spend their time dealing with selling the mobile home, you can help.

Medical costs may be so high that the owner cannot pay for the lot rent or for the normal maintenance of the mobile home. The owner may have to move in with her children. Perhaps the owner moved months ago and gave permission to a neighbor to sell her mobile home. Another reason the seller may want to move is that she is buying a regular house and needs the money from the sale of the mobile home as a down payment at the closing. Closing is coming up soon. The closer it gets to closing, the more desperate she is to sell her mobile home. She wants that cash and will take any cash you give her. She doesn't want to pay lot rent, and she doesn't want to be dealing with that mobile home anymore.

In looking for mobile homes you wish to purchase, you are interested in two and three bedroom mobile homes. More people want two and three bedroom mobile home. Why not a one bedroom mobile home? Take a look at the example at the beginning of the last chapter. That was a one bedroom mobile home. Even if your buyer only needs one bedroom, always be looking ahead. How easy will it be for that buyer to eventually sell the mobile home? There are fewer people that want a one bedroom mobile home. It is to that buyer's advantage in the future to purchase a two bedroom mobile home.

Ideally, you would like a mobile home built from the mid-1980s and newer. Sometimes mobile homes built in the late 1970s are okay, but not those built in the 1960s. They are not as safe as mobile homes manufactured since the 1980's. There are not that many of them around. They are smaller and have the possibility of more problems and resemble RVs from that time period, so you do not want to work with a 1960s mobile home.

What does your seller really want, and how can you help him? Initially of course, you will find out that he just wants cash, but as you listen to him, you might find out what he wants the cash for. I worked with a seller, let's call him Joe, who wanted cash for the mobile home he had already moved out of, but as I listened to Joe, I found what he really needed. He needed cash to pay for siding on the regular house he had moved into. Well it turned out that I knew someone who did siding, and my siding guy worked with insurance agencies. This particular regular house that Joe owned had a lot of dents from hail in it. I was able to connect these two together, saving my mobile home seller thousands of dollars because he got the siding paid for by his insurance company, minus a small deductible. I was also able to purchase his mobile home and sell to a new buyer whom I had previously identified.

It could be that the person does not want cash. I have seen plenty of people online who are looking to trade a mobile home for a four wheeler or a boat or an ATV. So if you happen to have one of those, and you want to trade it for a mobile home, it may work for you. I have not done that, but it might work for you.

Listening is the most important thing that you can do. One of the people I bought a mobile home from said, "So long as we have enough money to pay our Realtor." It's all a matter of what it is that the seller is looking for.

The last factor to consider is the marketability of the mobile home. Even if you have a buyer already in place for the mobile home, and you should, of course, you want to make sure the mobile home is marketable for the person you are selling it to, so when she wishes to sell it, it will be marketable. The location of the mobile home is very important. Does the industry in the area support jobs? Is it located in a one-company town? If it is a one-company town, and the company goes under, so does the mobile home park. Compare the lot rent to the rents of apartments and houses in the area. Is the lot rent much less than the rent for apartments and houses in the area? I try to save the people I work with $200-$400 a month. See if that is the case with the mobile home you are buying. The number of vacant mobile homes in the park is important to take note of. Look at the crime in the area. The park may be beautiful, but the crime around the area may be not what you are looking for. What is the condition in the park? Is it very good? Make sure it is well-maintained. These are important marketability points you will want to consider when choosing a mobile home for your buyer.

Now that you found the buyer, the seller and mobile home, you also want to make sure it is in a park that you are going to be able to work with. This is what the next chapter is about.

#4

PARK OWNERS AND MANAGERS WIN!
Who's In Need of monthly rent to support their business and improve their neighborhood? The Manufactured Home Park!

How and Why to Bring the Park Managers or Owners onto your Team

Your seller will be getting cash soon. Your buyer will be in her American Dream. What can you do for the park owners and managers that care for the land your buyer's mobile home will be on? How can you determine whether the park atmosphere where your buyer will be living is inviting? This chapter will show how to pick out the right mobile home park to work with, what these parks provide for your buyers and what you can do for them to meet their needs, because you want them to WIN too.

What parks are you searching for and what are the red flags? As mentioned in a previous chapter, you are looking for a park that is reasonably filled. If many of the mobile homes are empty, it could indicate negligent management or absentee ownership. Remember, you want to provide decent, affordable housing. If the park is not well cared for, it may not be a decent neighborhood. If many of the mobile homes are empty, it could also indicate high crime around the area. There was one park I worked with – a beautiful, beautiful park - very well maintained, clearly with a lot of pride of ownership in the park. The same family had owned the park for generations, but while they owned this park, the neighborhood around them was crumbling. The crime rate was soaring, the businesses were closing. The residents didn't want to live in a high crime area. They started moving out, so the management raised the lot rent to pay for the cost of maintaining the property and put more expensive mobile homes in the park, but it did not draw more people in. So, it is very important to investigate the crime statistics in the area to see if it has increased in the last few years or not.

The other reason that mobile homes could be empty in the park is that there could be a bad local economy. It could be that the town is dependent on one company for most of its workers. Most of those workers live in apartments or mobile homes, but if that factory closes, people will lose their jobs and leave. This may not be a park that meets your criteria. If you find a buyer for a mobile home in that park, you need to look ahead and make sure your buyer is well provided for, so that when he wants to sell his mobile home after the end of the note term, the mobile home is going to be in an area where he can resell it. You can do this by looking into the company's stability in the industry that it's in.

Although you can't predict what will happen ten or twenty years in the future, you can get a pretty good idea of the next few years. You want to set your clients up to succeed, not to fail. It is a good business practice to set your clients up to succeed. The better you take care of your buyers, your sellers, and your parks, the better business you have. Remember, the more needs you meet, the more you WIN, the more you profit.

Sometimes a park is too well cared for. I became aware of an example of this when I was shopping for a mobile home in a particular park for a buyer. The park seemed very nice inside; curbed streets, swimming pool, reasonable prices; until I found out that the park had security cameras everywhere. Privacy was minimal in this park. It was a gated community, but it was not a fancy gated community. It had a lot of older mobile homes in it. The manager told me that he checks every single mobile home to see how high the grass is getting, because he did not want the grass to get four inches high. In this park, the owners were in charge of their own lawns. He said that he had no problem with dropping a letter to fine the home owner, when their grass was too high. Actually, he seemed to relish the idea. The more he spoke, the more I realized that he was watching the daily lives of individual residents. He actually used the security cameras to literally watch the grass grow and watched the lives of the individuals living in the mobile homes in the park. That was just creepy to me and I did not want to deal with that park. So this is a park that I decided to avoid.

Parks that are friendly to what you are doing will call you instead of you feeling like you are begging to work in their park. You want the park managers to feel comfortable calling you if someone applies to live in the park, and could qualify for the park, but cannot afford to buy a mobile home by borrowing from a bank.

You are searching for a park that has standards for the mobile homes within the park; nothing extreme – just enough to respect the privacy of the owner and show that the management wants to keep up the neighborhood.

A park that owns and maintains the land better fits your criteria. These parks may rent a few mobile homes but the park owner does not want to hold the notes on these mobile homes. The park owner wants to collect lot rent every month. He does not want to hassle with the buying and selling of mobile homes. One park owner I talked to said that he collects lot rent in his mailbox every month. He added that, in his park, how the residents buy and sell their trailers is their business, not his.

Some park owners think of their mobile home park like a multi-unit apartment building: they rent all the mobile homes. A park that owns few of its mobile homes works best. Most of the park owners you will want to work with do not want to deal with renters, they want homeowners. Homeowners take better care of their mobile homes.

One of the reasons you want to work with a park that owns very few of its mobile homes, is because if you find it is a park you want to do business with, the park management may send you multiple leads. Contrary wise, if the park owns most of the mobile homes in the mobile home community, there are not going to be many leads for you. Also, your buyer wants to be in a park where she can own her own mobile home. You are not trying to find someone a mobile home to rent; you are looking for someone to buy the mobile home. You are providing the American Dream: the pride of home ownership.

What does a park provide for the buyer? Mobile home parks do provide many things for the lot rent charged every month. To begin with, lot rent covers paying to rent the land that the park owns. That is the biggest chunk of lot rent. The park owner had to purchase that land. The park owner pays taxes on that land every year, and the park owner maintains the land so that mobile homes may be placed on it.

Park owners, or managers, are responsible for everything from the ground down. This includes having water and sewer for everyone in the mobile home park. Not all mobile homes are near cities, so not all mobile homes have city water and sewer. Some of them have wells, some of them have septic systems, and some of them have other ways to dispose of waste. Regardless of the system, getting water to each home and providing for waste liquid from each mobile home is the responsibility of the park. Typically the park provides access to natural gas. Not all mobile homes have hookups for gas. Some of them have propane. Sometimes individual units have propane. The park also provides access to electricity for each unit.

The park takes care of common areas. The building and maintaining of streets in the mobile home park are provided by the park, whether those streets are concrete with curbs, asphalt or gravel. This could mean the park has the streets in the park plowed in the winter, if you are in the northern areas.

Some parks have common areas for people to walk their dogs in, like a little dog park. Some mobile home parks take care of your lawn, the little grassy area between your mobile home and the unit next to you. Other places leave you responsible to take care of the lawn yourself. Some mobile home parks even have a playground, a pool, and lakes with paddle boats, golf courses, a clubhouse, a basketball court, or a laundry building. Some have small resorts around them. All of these amenities are taken care of by the mobile home park. These are just some examples of what lot rent can cover, depending on the park.

Why is it important for you to have the mobile home park on your team? Both of you can keep each other informed if the new buyer is not paying. There was a situation I had with one buyer and her checks were bouncing and it was very strange, because she was not the type of person whose checks would bounce. It turned out this person had her identity stolen, twice. In this situation, I could see that the checks were bouncing and had talked to the buyer, who at this point did not understand what had happened. After a couple of months, I spoke with the manager of the park and let her know that I was having this situation. I expect her to do the same thing with me if the park manager has the same situation. As it turned out, the park management was not having the same problem that I was having. Once the identity thief situation was handled by proper authorities, the whole issue wrapped up in the next couple of weeks and I never had to deal with this again.

This is why communication with your buyer, even after she purchases your mobile home, is so very important. The more communication you have with your buyer, the more likely she is not going to walk away in the middle of the night, and you will continue to be paid month after month.

The park may be able to recommend someone to help if your mobile home has an issue, or perhaps someone on their staff can help you. When I had that mobile home that I was trying to sell for a year, I needed to replace the deck. The park was willing to build the deck for me to my specifications and at a fair price. They did an excellent job. During the winter I came out there at least once a week to make sure the pipes didn't freeze. The park manager contacted me, when the temperatures reached below freezing. The pipes had frozen. The management hired a heat-tape specialist to get the problem taken care of for me, without my being there. Your park management or park owner can be very helpful.

Parks screen your buyers. This is really beneficial for you. Before someone can live in a mobile home park, he has to be approved by the park management. The park will do a credit check, a criminal background check, contact the references and verify the applicant's employment. The Park management wants to make sure that the person living in the park is going to be able to pay lot rent every month. Because the mobile home park does all of these things, you don't have to do it as thoroughly. You just have to keep up good communications with the park. There is no point in having an applicant's background checked twice. The park does not have to share the information with you, but the management may give you general information about whether your buyer is much of a risk. For example, the park manager will let you know if your buyer is not approved by the park. With that being the case, you are done looking for mobile homes in that particular park for that particular buyer. Parks can only share so much with you legally as to why the buyer was not approved, but the park could generally say if the buyer's credit wasn't approved, or generally say there was a glitch on the criminal background check that was done on him. You want to work with parks that have standards as to who is actually allowed to be in the park. If the standard is too high then buyers may not qualify. Only one park I know of has actually asked for a credit score. Their lot rents were very high. I might have the right buyer for that park someday, but it would be rare. That particular park did understand what I was doing, and did want me to work with them. Unfortunately, most of their mobile homes were outside my price range.

Sometimes a park's standards are just too low. This could indicate that it is a dangerous place to live. There was one park some friends and I drove through that had signs in front that said 'NO GAMBLING' 'DO NOT LEAVE YOUR VEHICLE' 'NO FIREARMS.' There was no one in the office, nor did it appear that there had been anyone in that office for years. There were a lot of abandoned trailers all around and a couple of "beer-bellied" shirtless men, with their dogs, hanging out by one trailer glaring at us. It was kind of a scary park. The standards in this park did not fit my criteria. This is not a park I wanted to work with. I provide decent, affordable housing.

Another really important reason to have the park on your team, is that you will have eyes on your investment to see if it is well taken care of. If you develop a relationship with the park owner or manager, the manager is more likely to give you a call if something is going awry at the mobile home. If she sees that you are an asset to the park, and you could do more for the park, then you are more likely to do more deals in their park.

How does the mobile home park WIN (profit) when you are working on mobile home deals in their park? The park will be receiving regular lot rent again, because you have placed a new buyer in the park. The more you work with the park, the more the park can benefit from your placing more buyers in their park. Vacant mobile homes in a mobile home park could encourage criminal activity: from scavenging metal to violent crimes.

I have alluded, from time to time, that if a mobile home is vacant, critters could get into the home. Sometimes, animals crawl, dig, or chew underneath the skirting and form nests in the insulation. Skunks have been known to live under mobile homes. I know of a cat that lived underneath a mobile home and the woman who lived there was not aware of it until the cat came up into her home. Her dog was surprised. The mobile home had been vacant for a long time before she moved in. So, it is important to the park not to leave a mobile home vacant for a long period of time.

Vandals can get into mobile homes. I have seen mobile homes with gang signs on the sides of the mobile home or on the doors. Vagrants can get into mobile homes. I have been to a home where it was quite obvious that someone was living there, who was not the owner of the home. I saw a broken window and I saw a blanket on the floor. These are signs that someone was inhabiting the home. Unless the management is on top of this, and watching every single mobile home, they may not notice these things. If they do occur, it devalues the mobile home, it disturbs the neighbors and it really cheapens the mobile home park and the whole neighborhood. Your business can improve the neighborhood because you place quality buyers in mobile homes.

You are an asset to the park because of the way you vet new buyers for a mobile home in their park; the new home buyer will have pride in home ownership. You are not finding a renter, you are finding someone who will take good care of that asset and who is excited about living in a home of her own. You are bringing someone into the park with the right kind of attitude, someone who may be happy there for many years.

When you first get into this industry and discuss with parks what you do, many mobile home parks will say, "No, we don't do that." They think you want to rent the mobile home. They think you want to take money that they could have. They are very protective of their tenants; very, very protective. They have seen too many people straight out of real estate boot camp with no experience. The park's first gut reaction is always going to be, "No we don't do that." But "no" does not always mean "no." There was one park where I confessed, I was, in fact, straight out of real estate boot camp and I went in and I talked to the park manager. She was none too happy with me, and she told me, emphatically, "We don't do that thing here". A couple of years later, when I had a buyer, and I knew that was the perfect park for my buyer, I went in and talked to the park again. This time, I had experience behind me and it turned out that my buyer knew someone who knew the manager's brother. Sometimes that is what it takes and BOOM, we're in the park. So you never know. You might end up in a park that you did not expect to be in. So just because a park says "no" to you, keep it in the back of your mind. It might be the perfect park for one of your buyers.

So how can you develop a relationship with a park manager or owner? Certainly something like what I just mentioned where the manager and buyer knew someone in common is a great way to get your foot in the door, but that is uncommon. You will find that every single park has its own unique personality. As you visit different parks, you are learning more and more about mobile home parks. Whether you are buying in a park or just driving through, you will get a good idea of what these different personalities are like. Sometimes it is just the direct approach of going straight to the manager and letting her know what it is that you want to do. She usually says no, but sometimes she will say yes. Sometimes she understands, and when she does, those parks will be calling you and saying, "I have another buyer for you. Are you interested? Do you have investors set up?" It is a wonderful thing.

The other approach you can use I call the 'exclusivity approach'. Write a letter to the park that says that you only work with a limited number of parks. You give them qualifications for being one of the exclusive parks that you work with.

There are over 44,000 mobile home parks in the United States that you can contact.

For a list of all the mobile home parks in the United States, check out the bonuses at:

www.thebookonincreasingyourroi.com

You want to have relational capital with your park, your buyer and your seller, so you want to be honest with everyone. How you choose to act and what you choose to say to park managers may determine which parks will want to work with you.

Now you have your buyer, you have your seller, and your park is on board. It is time to negotiate and close. And that is what will be covered in the next chapter.

#5

TWO WINNERS!

Who's In Need of a great deal?

You and the Seller

Learning the Art of Negotiating and Closing

You have found a buyer and seller in need, and a mobile home for your buyer in a park that fits her needs, so let's wrap up the deal and WIN (profit). In this chapter, you will learn what to do once you've picked the perfect mobile home for your buyer, how to calculate how much to offer, how to negotiate for the optimum price and how to close the deal.

First, a little bit about the procedure in obtaining the mobile home. You have a buyer, you have a mobile home that is for sale, but ultimately you are going to be buying the mobile home for the buyer. So, the first thing you are going to do is go shopping for your buyer. Choose three mobile homes that suit your buyer's criteria. You prioritize the mobile homes based on what she has told you and based on how you think the numbers are going to work. **Always know the ending before you know the beginning in Real Estate. Calculate the numbers that will work, ahead of time.** There will be some hypothetical examples of numbers below. You have a very good idea as to what your buyer can afford. So, you show her the mobile homes you've picked. Preferably you only have to show her one mobile home, but if need be, you can show her the second or third one based on what needs and wants she has indicated. Once she has decided which mobile home she likes, or which one she prefers, you let her know that since you are going to be the one purchasing the mobile home, you are going to be the one who negotiates the deal for the mobile home. You will get her the best price possible, at the monthly payment that she can afford, that the two of you talked about already. You will let her know the results of your negotiations, as they relate to her monthly payment, within 24 hours. Meanwhile, if you think she will be living in this mobile home park, she can begin the application process with the park office. You go back to the seller and start to negotiate an actual price on the mobile home that you will pay cash for as soon as your buyer has been approved by the park. If the seller can't agree to a price that will work for you and your buyer, you move on to another seller. But you should have that price determined in advance, which is why you need to determine the Maximum Allowable Offer or MAO.

Let's talk about profit. As an investor, what is your time worth? Orchestrating deals such as shown in the example that follows takes time. You need to find and develop relationships with potential buyers, sellers, investors and park managers. You need to piece together a deal that is a 5-way win. The deal has to benefit the buyer, the seller and your investor. The park manager will benefit when he has a homeowner paying lot rent. Of course the deal has to work for you. That means your profit on the deal needs to be worth the time you put into it. The time it takes to set up, negotiate and implement one of these deals is significant. Not every deal goes through. And there are risks if you don't know what you're doing. That's why each deal needs to result in a substantial profit for you.

NUMBERS IN A DEAL
The Example

Variation #1
In this example lot rent is $500/mo. and the buyer's monthly income is $2,400.

The buyer's monthly housing cost should not exceed about 1/3 of his income, so he can afford $800/mo. Subtracting the $500 lot rent leaves $300 available for the note payment (that's the loan payment the buyer will pay you each month). In this example, your buyer can afford and is willing to pay you $300/month for 48 months.

You have found an investor willing to invest $6,000 in this deal, and you don't plan to use any of your own money. Your investor wants a 10% return. Amortizing this loan over 4 years (using a loan calculator app on your phone), you would make 48 payments of $152.18 to your investor (paying him a total of $7,305 over the 4 year period).

The seller is asking $9,500; however, you have only $6,000 available for this deal. In addition, you have agreed as part of this deal to pay for new appliances, needed repairs to the trailer skirting and heat tape that will cost a total of $1,500. So you can pay no more than $4,500 to the seller ($6,000 - $1,500). Will he sell for $4,500? Unless he has other buyers lining up outside waving cash, he very likely will take $4,500 (in large part to avoid continuing to owe lot rent to the park each month).

Now you already have a buyer lined up. Even if the buyer knows you are only paying $4,500 + $1,500 for the mobile home and repairs, he is OK with the deal because he does not have $6,000 cash, but he is happy to pay you $300/mo.

You buy the mobile home with cash from the investor. You sell the mobile home to your client for 48 monthly payments of $300. You have the buyer sign a promissory note to that effect. You make sure you are listed as the lien holder on the title. Using your loan calculator app you set the sale price at $10,123 and the loan at 18.5% interest. You can use any combination of sale price and interest rate that results in the agreed upon $300/month for 48 months.

Your net monthly cash flow is $300 minus the $152.18 payment to your investor, a net monthly cash flow of $147.82 for 48 months ($7,095 total profit). Sweet! You put no money of your own into the deal so your ROI is infinite. Your investment was the time to set up the deal. Your investor got what she wanted, a 10% return without using her own time to set up the deal. This investor receives 48 payments of $152.18 for a total of $7,305, a profit of $1,305 on her $6,000 investment. She is delighted, because her money was previously in a mutual fund earning less than 3% interest.

$$Your\ investor's\ ROI\ is: \frac{\$(7{,}305 - 6{,}000)}{\$6{,}000}$$

$$= \frac{\$1305}{\$6{,}000} = 0.21 = 21\%$$

$$Your\ ROI\ is: \frac{\$(7095 - 0)}{\$0} = \frac{\$7095}{\$0} = infinite$$

Variation #2

Not all investors are the same. In an alternate to the above example, your investor is willing to loan you $6,000, but instead of an amortized loan he expects $600 per year interest (10% per year) and he does not expect his principal back until the end of the 4 year loan. So you pay him $600 at the end of each of the first 3 years and $600 + $6,000 at the end of the fourth year. The investor makes more money this way ($600 x 4 = $2,400 vs. $1,305 in the previous example). You, of course, earn less ($14,400 total received in payments from buyer - $6,000 cost of mobile home - $2,400 interest to investor = $6,000 profit vs. $7,095 in the previous example). Still, that is a nice profit.

$$Your\ investor's\ ROI = \frac{\$(8,400 - 6,000)}{\$6000}$$

$$= \frac{\$2,400}{\$6,000} = 0.4 = 40\%$$

$$Your\ ROI\ is: \frac{\$(6,000 - 0)}{\$0} = \frac{\$6,000}{\$0} = infinite$$

Variation #3

In a third variation of this example, your investor wants to be a 50% equity partner in the deal. She will put up all the money ($6,000) and you will do all the work. The total income from the deal is $300 x 48 months = $14,400. The total cost is $6,000, so the total profit is $14,400 - $6,000 = $8,400. In this version of the example, your investor makes $4,200 and you make $4,200. Which is still a nice piece of change. Note that if you pay this investor back in equal monthly payments of ($6,000 principal + $4,200 his share of the profit) / 48 = $212.50 per month, she is actually earning the equivalent of a $6,000 loan amortized for 4 years at 29% interest!

$$Your\ investor's\ ROI = \frac{\$(10,200 - 6,000)}{\$6,000}$$

$$= \frac{\$4,200}{\$6,000} = 0.7 = 70\%$$

$$Your\ ROI\ is\ \frac{\$(4,200 - 0)}{\$0} = \frac{\$4,200}{\$0} = infinite$$

Variation #4

There is no one to invest with you. You put up all the money ($6,000) and do all the work. The total income from the deal is $300 x 48 months = $14,400. The total cost is $6,000, so the total profit is $14,400 - $6,000 = $8,400. Your profit is $8,400. AWESOME!

$$Your\ ROI\ is\ \frac{\$(14{,}400 - 6{,}000)}{\$6{,}000}$$
$$= \frac{\$8{,}400}{\$6{,}000} = 1.4 = 140\%$$

No matter how you and your investor work the numbers, your MAO (Maximum Allowable Offer) in this example is $4,500.

The Power of Listening

In order to determine the MAO, you would have had to have listened to the buyer and the seller, the investor and the park, and hopefully yourself to orchestrate a totally awesome deal where everyone WINs-everyone profits. I cannot emphasize enough the power of listening. If you listen and respect the seller, you will have met a new friend. It will look like the seller just wants money, but sometimes she wants something else. She may not be as blunt as to say, "I really need this money for_____". More than likely she will not actually say anything like that. As you get to know the seller, and a mutual trust builds between you, she may open up to you so you can see what her needs really are. You may be able to fulfill those needs, not just with the money she's receiving, but in other ways, too. Maybe the seller didn't know a particular government agency could help her with something, or she needed to know where her child could learn to swim. Even friendship can happen. I became friends with one of my sellers after I sold her mobile home. Since the deal, she became interested in real estate and we have had lots of fun in and out of Real Estate. You never know what you will get out of these deals. This business can give you returns in ways other than money.

Some mobile home investors I know of have done such a good job of conveying a sense of trust with the seller, that the seller just gives the investor the key to the mobile home and turned over the title to them without any exchange of money. Sometimes a seller is just looking for a little respect, someone to listen to her. There are also times when the seller will act hard-nosed and doesn't soften. The seller is not ready to sell yet. Nurture the relationship anyway, as best you can. She might refer you to someone else or soften later. As you are listening to the seller, you may realize that buying this mobile home might not be the best situation for you. The seller may be telling you about the atmosphere of the neighborhood or the park, the city that the park is located in, or perhaps the neighbors around where you were considering purchasing a mobile home. That may tell you this is not the right thing to do. Again, listening is very important. It fosters trust between the two of you, which fosters good relational capital, which allows everybody to win.

In negotiations, one of the questions you might ask is, "How low should I go without losing the negotiation?" While making an offer based on the asking price, I generally ask 20-40% below my maximum acceptable offer. So in the above example, I know I am going way below his asking price. 20% below my MAO in the above example would be $4,500 x 0.80 = $3,600. If I were asking 40% off the MAO, I would ask for $4,500 x 0.60 = $2,700. Take note of the issues with the mobile home and let the seller know you are trying to get the best deal you can for your friend. The seller knows you are paying for someone else's mobile home. It's okay to be uncomfortable for a little bit. The seller may say no, but he might surprise you and say yes, or he could counter exactly where you want the price to be, or lower.

Another important tool in negotiations is the power of silence. Say, "Would you take $3,600 for the mobile home?" Then permit silence. Uncomfortable silence. Feel the squirming in the room as the seller is trying to silently tell you he wouldn't take it, he shouldn't take it, and then he bursts out with an offer that may be even lower than your MAO. So silence is a really, really strong tool, but you have to be able to hold that silence long enough to allow the seller to actually put an offer out, because if you throw an offer out first, you will not get it as low as you really want it.

The mobile home shown in the first chapter was originally for sale at $18,000. It was for sale with a Realtor. I had someone with me who was going to help me with the negotiations. When I first saw the mobile home, I thought, "Oh, that's too nice of a mobile home. I don't think I can even bid on that mobile home." My friend got very excited because he likes negotiations. So, after talking to the owner for a while, my friend and I were ready to make an offer. As I said, the mobile home had just been on the market for $18,000 and the owner had dropped the price to $15,000. We didn't know that until later, though. What do you think my associate offered him for that mobile home? He offered $8,000. He said, "Would you take $8,000 cash today if I gave it to you right now?" And the silence in the room, you could touch it. No one said anything for the longest time. And although the owners didn't say anything, it was such a long time, you could feel everyone squirming. Everyone wanted to say something. And finally the silence was broken by the owner who could stand it no longer and said, "Would you consider ten?" Oh yeah, we would consider ten. That was lower than we had actually anticipated. So, we were very excited about that. It was that palpable silence that silence everyone could feel that made the negotiations effective. And after the silence was over, everyone was happy. But during that moment when everyone is squirming, it is very uncomfortable. It is just a matter of getting past that point, so that everyone can end up with the price that everyone wins at.

In all of this, don't lose sight of your own needs. Make sure it is always a win-win for you, the buyer, the seller and the mobile home park. Sometimes, your sellers and your buyers have drama surrounding them. It is easy to get caught up in the drama of the seller or of the buyer – Don't! Listen to the stories. Solve what you can, but don't get wrapped up in someone else's problems. Stay focused on your bottom line. Be prepared to walk away if you need to.

Closing:
The Handshake

Once the new buyer states a price at or below your MAO, immediately go for the handshake. Once that handshake has taken place, the deal is sealed and everyone knows it. Thank the seller, and mean it. Now you can talk about a closing date and prepare a bill of sale.

Repairs that may be needed for a mobile home have been touched on in the last few chapters. The next chapter goes into much more detail about those repairs.

#6
HANDYMEN AND WOMEN WIN!
Who's In Need of work? Handymen and women!

How to Evaluate What Must be Repaired and How to find the Right Person for the Job

You may know someone who does handyman work. If not, there are flyers at the grocery store, business cards at the paint stores, advertisements in newspapers and even magnets on cars advertising handymen. Some simply read: "Handyman call xxx-xxxx." Some ads that are more specific say: "Painting, carpentry, and electric - no job too small." I have seen: "We will repair what your husband fixed" and a handyman company called: "Rent-a-husband." The fact is you don't have to look far to see there are men and women who can help you when you need work done. If you purchase a mobile home that will need some work, you will first see if you can find a handyman to complete the tasks you need. Sometimes you will need an expert in that area, but for the most part, handymen and women will be able to get the job done. If you have not seen any of these ads, most big box hardware stores have a list of contractors. Paint stores often have a list of painters or a bulletin board with business cards. Collecting a list these names will be helpful. You never know when a need will come up. Having the names available can be helpful to your buyer or seller as well when he asks you: "Do you know a guy who….?" You will have a list of guys and gals that can help repair things around the mobile home.

Ideally, no repairs will be needed, but if repairs must be done immediately in order for your buyer to move in, the costs should not exceed the amount of money your investor has available, preferably not over 20% of the accepted offer on the mobile home. The mobile home must be livable as is, not dangerous. You buy mobile homes that may need minor work. You are not rehabbing!

The biggest red flag you will see when examining a mobile home for a buyer is water damage! Floors in mobile homes are made up of a substance similar to particle board. The walls are either made of drywall or paneling. The ceilings also are made of a substance that, when it gets wet, gets soggy. When the floors, ceilings or walls get wet, it can cause mold or dry rot. The floor can get spongy and eventually just fall through. Because of this situation, structural damage might result, so you need to find the source of the water damage. Look underneath the sinks; perhaps one of the sinks is leaking. The water could drip under the sink and spread to the subfloor. Look for soft spots in the floor anywhere, but especially near tubs, showers, toilets, and windows. It could be that one leaky faucet or toilet needs to be repaired and only a few floor boards need to be replaced and then all is well, but it is good to err on the side of caution.

If there are water stains on the ceiling, you could have a problem with the roof. Look under the window frames; the wall could be buckled or there could be a line of darkness below the windows that indicates that the seller tried to wipe it off, but there is still mold there. This would indicate that water is leaking in your windows when they are not open. Replacing the window, or even sealing it properly might be your only issue. You might check the outdoor water spigot. Is there any indication there is leakage under the mobile home? This is not as much of an issue because it does not usually damage the mobile home, unless there is a leak in the piping and there is water spraying up under the floorboards of the mobile home. Check the washing machine area to make sure that there is no water damage on the floor there. You might ask the owner where the main water valve is, not because you are going to need it, but the end buyer may need it at some point, and it is good to be able to tell him how to shut off the water in case of a water emergency.

Other repairs to look for are electrical. Take a look at the electrical box. Inside every electrical box in mobile homes, there should be an indicator as to what part of the United States that mobile home itself should be placed in. Make sure the mobile home is built for the climate it is located in. Also check to see if the electrical box is old. Check outlets. Are they broken or blackened? Do all the circuits work? This is not usually an issue, but it is good to be sure.

Check for the stability of the mobile home itself. Is the home level? I like to do a pencil test. When I am talking to the seller at the kitchen counter top, I place a pencil on the counter top to see if it rolls. It's a pretty easy test, and no one has to know you are testing anything. Another test involves just bringing in a glass of water, an open glass of water, not one with a lid on it where you can see if the water is level. Place it on the counter top and see what happens to the water. Does it remain straight? Does it tilt? A friend of mine uses an app on his phone to check how level a mobile home is. Mobile homes can be adjusted because they are resting on piers or cinderblocks underneath and those can be adjusted. That can be a little expensive, maybe $500-750.

Find out when the roof was last replaced or repaired. There are several kinds of roofs for mobile homes. Very old mobile homes with flat roofs may have a tar and gravel roof. The rubber roof, also called a membrane roof, can also be found on older mobile homes. They are relatively easy to replace and one of the least expensive roofs. It definitely keeps the water out. Metal roofs are also inexpensive. They are just so very loud when it rains. They need to be inspected for signs of corrosion. Finally, there is the traditional asphalt roof with shingles like on a regular house. These are much more expensive, but they are becoming more common in mobile home parks.

Another repair you want to check on, in the northern regions of the United States, is heat tape over the piping. Water pipes underneath the mobile home are exposed to outdoor air temperature. The skirting does not insulate them. Although there is some insulation under a mobile home, it is not enough to prevent pipes from freezing. If the pipes freeze, anything water dependent is not functional. Eventually, the pipes will burst, and this can be a very expensive repair. Heat tape is placed around the pipes and is thermostat controlled. When the pipes hit a certain temperature, the heat tape will automatically begin to heat the pipe. Some heat tape is manually controlled and it must be turned on from in the mobile home. The mobile home owner must be aware of outdoor temperature variables. When it gets to be under, say, 39 degrees at night, the resident flips a switch on and then the heat tape will go on. It can be kept on until spring. Unfortunately, the switch may look like a regular wall switch, so it is easy to forget what it is and turn it off during winter by accident.

Some mobile homes need exterior paint or stain. Some of the older mobile homes, like the one I mentioned previously, have metal siding; some have wood sides. Today, most mobile homes have vinyl siding, so you don't need to worry about painting it.

Something that was very popular for many years inside mobile homes was paneling. Back in the 60s and 70s, and even in the 80s, paneling was on all the walls. Many of these mobile homes still have paneling on their walls. If you can paint that paneling a light color, a cream color, ecru, an off-white of some sort, it really brightens the room and makes what could appear to be cramped quarters look larger.

When shopping for a mobile home for your client, you might find a good mobile home, but the deck may be pretty awful. Maybe it is just a rattling little metal thing sitting in front of the door, or the wooden boards bend too much under your feet. Is it safe to get in and out of the mobile home? You might want to think about getting a nice wooden deck built for the safety of your buyer. If this repair is the only thing holding her back from buying the mobile home, add it to her loan without increasing the amount of her monthly payments by just adding a few more months to her loan. Providing safe, decent, affordable housing at a price your buyers can afford is what you do.

Look at the heating and air conditioning units. Does the mobile home have central air? Are there window air conditioners? If not, you may want to pick up at least one used window unit for the mobile home. When was the last time the units were serviced? How old are they? These are questions to ask the seller.

Some mobile homes need cosmetic repair. What first catches your eyes when you are about to look at a mobile home? Probably you will notice the front of the mobile home, the deck, the siding on the mobile home, and the skirting on the mobile home. Does the siding have any major damage? Examine the area to see how extensive the damage is and if it needs to be repaired before selling the home to the end buyer. The mobile home does not have to be in perfect shape; in fact, it likely will not be. Skirting is the plastic or vinyl that goes from the bottom of the mobile home to the ground. The skirting serves two purposes: it makes the mobile home look classier and it keeps all the large critters out. This way, you won't have the raccoons or skunks crawling around in there chewing on the heat tape or building nests inside your insulation. If you see that the skirting is damaged or missing, especially near the hot water heater, or other piping areas, you may want to mention this to the seller. He may just want to drop his price again. As a side note, I should mention, on older mobile homes, the hot water heater is often accessible from a little door on the outside.

Check the fixtures in the mobile home, make sure every single faucet turns on and water comes out, and every single toilet flushes. Make sure the washing machine actually works.

If you see a lot of little things around the mobile home that could be repaired, but don't really reduce the mobile home's value that much, don't worry about it. Just leave that up to the buyer to take care of. A mobile home is a very inexpensive place to live. It doesn't have to be perfect. Only add to the buyers new note repairs that really must be taken care of. You don't want to spend money on all new windows, flooring, carpeting or painting the whole interior, or little things like door knobs and décor. You don't need to spend money staging the mobile home because you already have a buyer. Why don't you want to spend money on these items? These are rehabbing tasks and you are not rehabbing the mobile home. You are finding a decent mobile home that your buyer can live in, not doing a fix and flip.

As time goes on, continue to gather a list of handymen that have experience in mobile homes, whether it is in painting, putting in appliances, flooring, or other specific tasks. A mobile home is different than a regular house in many ways; your handyman should be well aware of these differences. Many things in a mobile home are lighter than in a standard house because the mobile home is perched on piers. It is not sitting on a foundation like a regular house. When hiring a handyman, do not pay in advance. There are too many stories of handymen who take full payment up front and never show up for the job, or only partially finish the job. Certainly a down payment for materials is acceptable, so that the handyman can get the materials for your job. Also, when looking for a handyman, ask for and check his references. One of the places that I have found handymen and contractors is the parking lot of Home Depot at 6:30 a.m. If you get there at 6:30 a.m. there will be lots of contractors there who are picking up supplies for a job they are currently working, and you can determine which ones have experience in mobile home parks and which ones do not. I just knock on their car doors and ask. As with anything else, trust, then verify.

The mobile home park that you are working with might also have a recommendation of handymen. Do be careful of this, though, because sometimes mobile home parks can be self-serving and over charge you. Sometimes, however, it can be very convenient and very helpful. I have taken advantage of that a couple of times when I have been in a situation where I was not local and had to have a repair or maintenance issue taken care of right away. The park may also recommend residents of the park, which helps build the very local economy.

There are many people you have helped so far. As has been stated throughout the book, as you look for who is in need and you are able to fulfill those needs, many people are winning, and many people are profiting; not just yourself, but others as well. So far the buyers have profited, the sellers have profited, the park has profited and the handymen and handywomen have profited. You are bringing profit to so many people including yourself in this business. It is very rewarding. But what if.....? That's what will be covered in the next chapter...

#7
Who WINS? Can I win? What if...?

Some Basic FAQs Answered

You have no lawyers involved, no bankers involved and usually no Realtors involved. But what if.. . .?

The biggest What if, of course, is what if the buyer stops paying?

Communication is the key in business, and it certainly is the key in this business. Let your buyer know to keep that line of communication open at closing or before, so that she is comfortable talking to you if something comes up. When you see that your buyer is having issues paying, whether she is skipping a payment or paying late, give her a call. Go over and talk to her. Reassure her, that you both may be able to work it out. Maybe you can modify the loan, or extend it. You and your investor or your equity partner have control as to what you want to do with that loan.

If the buyer has been paying all the time, and you have been communicating with her, normal business communication might be enough to prevent a problem. I send a statement every month, stating what my client owes on the note, and thanking her for payment from last month. Also, my statements show clearly how much interest and principal has been paid. It also looks professional. Sending a statement acknowledging that payment has not been received and that a late payment has accrued usually is enough to nudge the client to send payment.

Simply checking in on your client every so often, to make sure everything is okay in addition to keeping your line of communication open, continues to establish the relationship you have fostered with her. This goes a long way in preventing nonpayment. It depends on the particular buyer as to how much you will need to communicate. One to three times a year is usually adequate. If she knows communication is always open, right from the beginning, and you have been working with this buyer for a bit now, and she trusts you, then she will communicate with you when something goes awry.

If she doesn't contact you about the problems with payment, call her and say, "I am just checking in with you because I haven't received your payment yet this month and your payment has always been on time. Is everything okay?" Then listen. Give the person your time and your ear. It's embarrassing to admit that she can't make the payment. So allow her to open up. If it is appropriate, ask more questions about employment, the family, possibly her health, etc. She will probably let you know what is going on. Perhaps something happened and she is not able to pay as much every single month. She will think that she will have to move out and all is lost, but she is dealing with you, and not some bank. Modify the loan. Extend it out longer. Most importantly, talk to her and find out if there is something you can do. I am not saying just forgive the loan. You need to reiterate that she has an obligation to you. It can be worked out. Be compassionate, but do not get caught up in the drama of your buyer. Ultimately, it is her issue, not yours. You can probably work it out and you will probably continue to receive payments, likely until the loan has been paid off. If your buyer has only two or three payments left, maybe it makes sense to forgive the rest of the loan. Each situation is unique. Assess your situation to see what makes sense to you.

At closing, encourage the buyer to contact you if a problem comes up before it becomes an issue. I would rather work with someone who lets me know ahead of time that there is an issue so we can solve the problem together, instead of the buyer just assuming there is nothing I can do to help her. I encourage my buyers to take initiative in this area and let them know how important communication is.

What if your buyer has been reliable up until this point, always paying the full amount on time and just frankly tells you she can't pay anymore?

Talk to your buyer. Communication with everyone is really important. But if you talk to her again and she just says, "I can't do it anymore" and she has been really good, paying for a while, you say to her, "I completely understand. Why don't I give you some money for moving expenses? I will let you go on your way." With that you give her the equivalency of one or two house payments in cash, once you have seen that she has left the mobile home in good condition. She then signs the title off to you, so you are no longer just a lien holder, you are now the owner of this mobile home and you can sell that mobile home again. This is a good practice. You may be short financially for a month or two, but you'll get another buyer, another loan, and you will make that money up very quickly – in two or three payments. If she can't pay the lot rent and she can't pay you anymore, and she does not know what else she can do, help her out as best you can. Exchange this help for the keys and title to the mobile home. Although legally you could repossess the home, this arrangement is much better for both parties.

What if there has been no communication, and you have tried, but the buyer is not communicating, not paying and in fact has snuck out in the middle of the night?

You have a first lien position on this mobile home. So if she leaves and stops paying the loan, you will have to speak to a lawyer, and go through the legalities of making the mobile home yours. At that point, you will be able to repossess the mobile home, resell it to another buyer and begin the whole process all over again.

What if the buyer is continuously paying late?

Ask the buyer if the due date still works for them or if an alternate date would work better. Quite often, this solves the problem.

What if the note is just too much hassle?

You don't want to deal with it anymore! You could sell the note. There are people out there who buy notes. These note buyers usually buy notes at a discount, so you sell it at a discount. You know where your profit margin has been in this deal and must decide how much you are willing to give up to not deal with this note anymore. You sell the note, and you get the cash. The note buyer now has the note and the lien to the mobile home and you are completely out of the picture.

What if the person has to move?

If he has to move and it is early in the process, you can arrange to sell the mobile home to another buyer and have that new buyer assume the loan of the person who is there. This is a fairly easy process. The original buyer writes out a bill of sale to the new end buyer. The loan will then be restructured for the new buyer, and the old buyer sells the mobile home to the new buyer for what she owes on the loan, and everybody is happy. You have a promissory note with the new buyer. But what if you don't find a new buyer right away? Well, it is very important to make clear to the current note holder that she is responsible for continuing to make payments until a new buyer is found. Let her know it is actually her responsibility to find a new buyer, but you will also be looking. Then you will do all you can to work with the current buyer to find a new buyer for her mobile home. That will benefit everyone. It is good business, and it is ethically the right thing to do.

What if your buyer dies?

Her heirs are responsible to pay you until the note is paid off. If the note is almost paid off, you could just forgive the loan. Again, this is a good business practice. If the buyer was that close to paying it off, it just makes sense. Furthermore, the heirs could potentially refer you to someone interested in doing business with you. Of course, if the heirs don't plan on keeping the mobile home, you can offer to buy it from them. For example, if the mobile home is worth about $8,000 retail and the buyer owed $2,000 on the loan, you could offer to buy it from them for $4,000. At closing the heirs receive $2,000 cash ($4000-$2000 for the remaining loan amount). The heirs are delighted to be rid of the mobile home, the loan, and have cash in their hands, hassle free. Now you can turn around and sell the mobile home for $8,000 to $10,000 to a new buyer on a new loan.

What if the mobile home burns down?

I have a clause in my agreement with each of my buyers stating that she must purchase mobile home insurance. Furthermore, in that insurance policy, I must be listed as the "loss payee" on the insurance policy. This is one of the conditions of the loan. If this condition is not met, the loan could be considered in default. The insurance company provides me updates as to whether my buyer has kept her insurance policy in force. When I get word that the policy is no longer in force, I give the buyer a call and make sure it is renewed. As a "loss payee", if the mobile home does burn down, the insurance company will pay the loan off first, so I get paid first, then they will pay any remaining damages to the owner. **It is of utmost importance to have this insurance clause in your loan agreement.**

Well, that should take care of most of the "What if's?" so let's get on with the closing.

#8
YOU, THE BUYER AND THE SELLER WIN!
Who's In Need of a professionally presented closing?
The Buyer, the Seller and You

How to Set Yourself Apart as a Professional. The t's to Cross and i's to Dot in a Professional Closing Experience

At this point, everyone has agreed in principle to the sale and the buyer has been approved by the park. Now it is time to close. You have presented yourself in a professional manner throughout this entire process. You have been respectful and you have shown that you know what you are doing, and this continues through the closing process. The buyer and the seller will be depending on your knowing more than they do. It is very important that you do know more than they do, and that you come across professionally.

Let me tell you a story of a not so professional closing. I saw a mobile home I wanted to purchase that was for sale with a Realtor. I called the Realtor on the sign and he came right over to show me the mobile home. The owner was at home. I liked the mobile home and decided to make an offer on the spot. The asking price was $17,000. In the middle of negotiating the deal with the owner, it got to the silent point of the negotiations. A low number, well below my $10,000 maximum, had just been thrown out there for the seller to consider. It was silent for a long time. Who couldn't take the squirm time? Who was the first to say something? The Realtor, who represented the seller, the one who was told in confidence what her bottom line was and had that number on a sheet of paper next to him. He said, "Well on this sheet, it says here that she will take as little as $12,000......" He totally gave it away. The seller glared at him. We continued the negotiations without his help and obtained the mobile home for less than the seller's "bottom line".

The Realtor had a little dog and he brought this little dog with him everywhere. So when he showed me the mobile home, he brought the little dog with him. The whole time he was at the mobile home, he had his dog with him. Was he carrying his little dog? No, he let his little dog run around inside the mobile home, which was a very well cared for home with this beautiful white carpet. He said, "Well I don't think my little dog has ever gone potty in a house before." As soon as he said that, the rest of us thought, "We don't want him to start now!" We all took turns carrying that little dog through the negotiations. We were not taking any chances. Anyway, the deal did go through, and we did close with the Realtor. The closing took place at the Realtor's office, and of course, he had his little dog with him. The little dog was running around in the room, where we were closing on the deal. The Realtor had a pile of paperwork related to the closing. This little dog just jumped up on the table and sat on all the paperwork. This is an example of a completely unprofessional closing. Yes, the Realtor had the papers and he had the knowledge, but was not professional. So time to dot those i's and cross those t's and do it right.

The Closings- General Procedures

Closing 1- You Buy the Mobile Home: A Scenario

You and the Seller have agreed on a price for the mobile home. For this example, let's say you both agreed to $5,000 and have agreed that the closing will take place at the mobile home.

On the day of closing, you do one last inspection of the mobile home. Until the papers are signed, it is not too late to back out, especially if you find something majorly wrong with the mobile home.

The Seller must have with him: the title, proof from the county office that the title is clear and the keys to the mobile home.

As the Buyer, you must bring: $5,000 cash and a receipt book. You could also bring two (maybe three in case of an error) blank copies of the bill of sale.

Procedure:
1) Fill out and go over two copies of the Bill of Sale. Have the Seller sign the Bill of Sale first, then you, as the Buyer, sign it.

2) Seller signs The Title over to you, and gives you proof from the county of a clean title.

3) You give seller $5,000 cash and fill out a receipt for payment with a copy so you both have proof of payment.

4) Seller gives you the keys. You now briefly own the mobile home.

5) Discuss coordinating the utilities with the seller so the utilities seamlessly shut off and turn on the same day from your seller to your buyer. Do not suggest the utilities be in your name.

TAKE NOTE: Make sure your buyer has been approved by the park before the 1st closing or you could be stuck with the mobile home, the lot rent, and utility payments, until you get a new buyer.

After the closing: You make a copy of both sides of the signed title. You keep that copy for yourself. You go to the Motor Vehicle Department with the original title signed over to you and the proof from the county that the title is clean.

Closing 2- You Sell the Mobile Home: A Scenario (continued)

You and the Buyer have agreed on a price for the mobile home. For this example, let's say you both agreed to $10,000 and have agreed that the closing will take place at the mobile home, preferably later in the day after the first closing.

As the Seller, you must bring with you: a copy of the signed title (proving that the actual title is in process and you are the current owner of the mobile home) and the keys to the mobile home.

As the Lien Holder, you bring to the closing: the promissory note and the amortization chart. Also you will bring an example of the first month's bill.

As a courtesy, you will also bring with you: Handy information for the Buyer: the address and hours of the nearest DMV, county treasurer's office' address and hours, utility information for gas and electric (water is arranged for by the park), and the name and contact information for the nearest mobile home insurance agent (I usually recommend Foremost as they specialize in mobile homes).

Procedure:
1) Go over and have the Buyer sign a Promissory Note for $10,000:
   a. Go over late fees, default clause, insurance and "loss payee" section, etc.
   b. Discuss how payment will be made (electronic auto-withdrawal, check, money order, etc.). Cash is not an option as it cannot be mailed and you will not drive to the mobile home every month for payment. Give buyer a copy of the first bill (due two months after closing).
   c. If a down payment is made on the mobile home, it is collected at this time and a receipt is issued.

2) Fill out and sign two copies of the bill of sale. Be sure to go over the whole Bill of Sale with the buyer, especially the "as- is" clause. As the seller, you sign first, then the buyer signs.

3) As the title is still being processed in your name, you may want to create a form giving the Buyer permission to live in the home until such time as the title comes in and can be placed officially in his name. This form can be given to the park office, if necessary.

4) Give the Buyer a sheet of paper with: the address and hours of the nearest DMV, county treasurer's office' address and hours, utility information for gas and electric (water is arranged for by the park), and the name and contact information for the nearest mobile home insurance agent.

5) Talk to Buyer about coordinating utilities as you have discussed it with previous owner.

6) You give the new Buyer the keys. They are now the proud owner of the American Dream, a home of his own. Well, almost.

7) The second part of the closing will take place as soon as your title is processed. Find out when the buyer is available in about two weeks to complete the closing during business hours when the motor vehicle department is open.

After closing, you wait for your title to come in the mail declaring you are the owner of the mobile home. Once you have received the title in your name, you go to the county office to get the form stating that you have paid taxes, then contact Buyer for part two of closing 2. Coordinate the closings so you never have to personally pay taxes.

Closing 2- Part Two -You Sell the Mobile Home- The DMV Paperwork: A Scenario (continued)

You and the Buyer go to the DMV. This will give you a chance to chat with your Buyer after he has moved in. Ask if the utilities worked out seamlessly. Ask if mobile home insurance has been purchased yet, and if so, are you written into the policy as the "loss payee".

Procedure:
1) At the DMV, sign the title over to your new Buyer.
2) Make sure that you are listed as the lien holder on the title of the mobile home.

The title will come to you in the mail, as the lien holder. Send a copy to your buyer and the mobile home park. This will let the park know who the owner is and who the lien holder is.

Send some flowers or a gift card to your new buyer, welcoming them to their new home.

CONGRATULATIONS!

You have finished your first mobile home deal.

Now you will receive a check or money order in the mail, month after month.

Below are samples of the documents required at the closings:

CERTIFICATE OF TITLE

INDIANA CERTIFICATE OF TITLE

STATE OF INDIANA
CERTIFICATE OF TITLE FOR A VEHICLE

MAKE	MODEL NAME	YEAR	VIN
SKY	1666	1991	

TITLE TYPE	FORMER TITLE/STATE	PURCHASE DATE	BODY TYPE
NORMAL			MH

	USAGE TAX PAID	ISSUE DATE
OWNER(S) NAME	$0.00	

ODOMETER/BRAND
EXEMPT/EXEMPT

MAILING ADDRESS   **BRAND(S)**

PHOENIX HOME ENTERPRISES LLC
PO BOX 9234
AURORA IL 605989234

SECOND LIENHOLDER

ADDITIONAL OWNER(S)   **LIEN RELEASED BY:**

X _____

PRINTED NAME: POSITION:

DATE: _____

FIRST LIENHOLDER   **THIRD LIENHOLDER**

PHOENIX HOME ENTERPRISES LLC
PO BOX 9234
AURORA IL 605989234

LIEN RELEASED BY: **LIEN RELEASED BY:**

X _____   X _____

PRINTED NAME: POSITION: PRINTED NAME: POSITION:
DATE: DATE:

The Commissioner of the Bureau of Motor Vehicles, pursuant to the laws of the State of Indiana, certifies that the vehicle/watercraft has been duly titled and the owner of the described vehicle/watercraft is subject to the liens set forth.

INDIANA BUREAU OF MOTOR VEHICLES
R. Scott Waddell, Commissioner

TITLE NUMBER

(1)

DO NOT ACCEPT TITLE SHOWING ANY ERASURES, ALTERATIONS OR MUTILATIONS

Front Page

PLEASE TYPE OR PRINT INFORMATION

REQUIREMENTS: Federal and State law requires that you state the mileage in connection with the transfer of ownership. Failure to complete, or providing false statement may result in fines and or imprisonment.

TO SELLER: Seller is responsible for completing form. If title is in more than one name, all owners listed on the title must sign as seller. Do not sign as a Seller until all areas of the assignment are completed. Any person signing for a company must state position.

TO PURCHASER: You must apply for a new certificate of title within thirty-one days of the date of purchase, or pay a delinquent penalty fee. All liens shown on the face of this title must be released before you apply for a new title.

We swear or affirm that the information on this form is correct. We understand that a false statement may constitute the crime of perjury.

I (We) certify to the best of my (our) knowledge that the odometer now reads and is the ACTUAL MILEAGE of the vehicle unless one of the following statements is checked.

		No Tenths
		MILES

☐ The odometer reading stated is in excess of its mechanical limits.

☐ The odometer reading is not the actual mileage. WARNING - ODOMETER DISCREPANCY

SELLER INFORMATION

Signature of Seller	Position (if applicable)
Signature of Seller	Position
Printed Name of Seller	Dealer Number (if applicable)
Printed Name of Seller	

Date of Sale (month, day, year)/Selling Price	Trade in Price (if any)/Total Price Paid

PURCHASER INFORMATION

Name of Purchaser		Dealer Number
Address		
City	State	Zip Code
Name of Lienholder (if applicable)		
Address		
City	State	Zip Code

☐ I AM AWARE OF THE ABOVE ODOMETER CERTIFICATION MADE BY THE SELLER(S)

Signature of Purchaser	Printed Name of Purchaser

FIRST RE-ASSIGNMENT BY REGISTERED DEALER ONLY

I certify to the best of my knowledge that the odometer reading is the ACTUAL MILEAGE of the vehicle unless one of the following statements is checked.

☐ The odometer reading stated is in excess of its mechanical limits.
☐ The odometer reading is not actual mileage. WARNING ODOMETER DISCREPANCY.

Name of Dealership	
Signature	
Printed Name	
Position	Dealer Number
Date of Sale (month, day, year)	

Name of Purchaser		Dealer Number
Address		
City	State	Zip Code
Name of Lienholder (if applicable)		
Address		
City	State	Zip Code

☐ I AM AWARE OF THE ABOVE ODOMETER CERTIFICATION MADE BY THE SELLER(S)

Signature of Purchaser	Printed Name of Purchaser

SECOND RE-ASSIGNMENT BY REGISTERED DEALER ONLY

I certify to the best of my knowledge that the odometer reading is the ACTUAL MILEAGE of the vehicle unless one of the following statements is checked.

☐ The odometer reading stated is in excess of its mechanical limits.
☐ The odometer reading is not actual mileage. WARNING ODOMETER DISCREPANCY.

Name of Dealership	
Signature	
Printed Name	
Position	Dealer Number
Date of Sale (month, day, year)	

Name of Purchaser		Dealer Number
Address		
City	State	Zip Code
Name of Lienholder (if applicable)		
Address		
City	State	Zip Code

☐ I AM AWARE OF THE ABOVE ODOMETER CERTIFICATION MADE BY THE SELLER(S)

Signature of Purchaser	Printed Name of Purchaser

THIRD RE-ASSIGNMENT BY REGISTERED DEALER ONLY

I certify to the best of my knowledge that the odometer reading is the ACTUAL MILEAGE of the vehicle unless one of the following statements is checked.

☐ The odometer reading stated is in excess of its mechanical limits.
☐ The odometer reading is not actual mileage. WARNING ODOMETER DISCREPANCY.

Name of Dealership	
Signature	
Printed Name	
Position	Dealer Number
Date of Sale (month, day, year)	

Name of Purchaser		Dealer Number
Address		
City	State	Zip Code
Name of Lienholder (if applicable)		
Address		
City	State	Zip Code

☐ I AM AWARE OF THE ABOVE ODOMETER CERTIFICATION MADE BY THE SELLER(S)

Signature of Purchaser	Printed Name of Purchaser

NO ADDITIONAL RE-ASSIGNMENTS PERMITTED

Back Page

Lori Robinson

MOBILE HOME BILL OF SALE

STATE OF ____ILLINOIS_____COUNTY OF_____LAKE_____

_____ ("SELLER") and

_____ ("BUYER") agree as follows:

For the payment of the sum of $_____ by BUYER and other good and valuable consideration, the receipt and sufficiency of which is hereby acknowledged, SELLER does hereby sell, transfer, and convey to BUYER and his heirs, executors, administrators, and assigns the following described mobile home:

Make: North American_____   **Model:**_____

Manufacturer:_____   **Serial Number:**_____

Year: 1979   **Size:**   840 SF   **Mileage:**   N/A_____

Current Location of Mobile Home:_____

_____

_____

Home is to be financed in accordance with terms and conditions of the promissory note dated _____ between the Buyer and Seller.

The mobile home listed in this bill of sale form is sold together with an equal interest in all fixtures, equipment, accessories, and all other necessaries thereto appertaining and belonging except:

_____

_____

_____

_____

SELLER hereby warrants that (s)he is the lawful owner of said mobile home and that (s)he has full legal right, power, and authority to sell said mobile home. SELLER further warrants said mobile home to be free of all encumbrances, liens, security agreements, claims, demands, and charges of every kind whatsoever and will warrant and defend the title to said mobile home against any and all persons whomsoever.

The said mobile home is being sold "as is" without any express or implied warranty as to condition or working order. There is no warranty for any defect and all repairs are the responsibility of the BUYER unless the SELLER indicates any repairs for which he/she/they will pay and be responsible for. If any repairs are to be made by the SELLER they will be listed here:

It is agreed that repairs to the mobile home as listed below (circle one) will / will not be made, and that the following accessories, upgrades, and/or aftermarket parts (circle one) will / will not be included:

SELLER and BUYER declare under penalty of perjury that to the best of their knowledge all disclosures to each other in connection with the above transaction, and all other information on this Bill Of Sale, is true and correct.

IN WITNESS WHEREOF, the Parties have executed this Bill Of Sale on this ____ day of

_____, 20____.

Seller Name(s):_____

Seller Signature(s):_____

Seller Street Address(es):_____

City:_____ State:_____ Zip Code: _____

Date Signed:_____

Buyer Name(s):_____

Buyer Signature(s):_____

Buyer Street Address(es):_____

City:_____ State:_____ Zip Code: _____

Date Signed:_____

Lori Robinson

PROMISSORY NOTE

Date:

Borrower:

Borrower's Address:

Payee:

Place for Payment:

Principal Amount:

Term:

Monthly Payments:

INTEREST RATE:

PAYMENT TERMS. This Note is due and payable as follows, to-wit:___monthly payments of _____. The first such payment due and payable on the _____, and a like installment shall be due and payable on the same day of each succeeding month thereafter until the total principal of _____ is paid in full. If each payment is not paid by the 5th of the month, a late fee of $10.00 per day will be assessed for every day it is late. PARTIAL PAYMENTS WILL NOT BE ACCEPTED. In addition, should Borrower make any payment with a check, returned because of insufficient funds, Payee shall have the right to charge $35.00 for each check returned. After the second time the Borrower's check is returned, Borrower must thereafter secure a cashier's check or money order for payment of Note.

BORROWER'S PRE-PAYMENT RIGHT. Borrower reserves the right to prepay this Note in whole or in part, prior to maturity, without penalty.

PLACE FOR PAYMENT. Borrower promises to pay to the order of Payee at the place for payment and according to the terms for payment the principal amount stated above. All unpaid amounts shall be due by the final scheduled payment date.

DEFAULT AND ACCELERATION CLAUSE. If Borrower defaults in the payment of this Note or in the performance of any obligation including Space Rental Agreement with the park, the default continues after Payee gives Borrower notice of the default and the time within which it must be cured, as may be required by law or written agreement, then Payee may declare the unpaid principal balance and earned interest on this Note immediately due. Borrower and each surety, endorser, and guarantor waive all demands for payment, presentation for payment, notices of intentions to accelerate maturity, notices of acceleration of maturity, protests, and notices of protest, to the extent permitted by law. If Borrower defaults on this note, Borrower agrees to release entire deposit made to park office to the Payee.

INTEREST ON PAST DUE INSTALLMENTS AND CHARGES. Interest on past due installments and charges will accrue at the interest rate shown in page 1 of this agreement.

INSURANCE The Buyer must maintain current home owners insurance to cover at least the amount owed to the Seller on the above property. The Buyer agrees to name the Seller as the First Lien Position and list the Seller as the "Loss Payee." The Buyer agrees to pay all property taxes on home.

FORM OF PAYMENT. Any check, draft, Money Order, or other instrument given in payment of all or any portion hereof may be accepted by the holder and handled in collection in the customary manner, but the same shall not constitute payment hereunder or diminish any rights of the holder hereof except to the extent that actual cash proceeds of such instruments are unconditionally received by the payee and applied to this indebtedness in the manner elsewhere herein provided.

ATTORNEY'S FEES. If this Note is given to an attorney for collection or enforcement, or if suit is brought for collection or enforcement, or if it is collected or enforced through probate, bankruptcy, or other judicial proceeding, then Borrower shall pay Payee all costs of collection and enforcement, including reasonable attorney's fees and court costs in addition to other amounts due.

SEVERABILITY. If any provision of this Note or the application thereof shall, for any reason and to any extent, be invalid or unenforceable, neither the remainder of this Note nor the application of the provision to other persons, entities or circumstances shall be affected thereby, but instead shall be enforced to the maximum extent permitted by law.

BINDING EFFECT. The covenants, obligations and conditions herein contained shall be binding on and inure to the benefit of the heirs, legal representatives, and assigns of the parties hereto.

DESCRIPTIVE HEADINGS. The descriptive headings used herein are for convenience of reference only and they are not intended to have any effect whatsoever in determining the rights or obligations under this Note.

CONSTRUCTION. The pronouns used herein shall include, where appropriate, either gender or both, singular and plural.

GOVERNING LAW. This Note shall be governed, construed and interpreted by, through and under the Laws of the State of _____.

Borrower is responsible for all obligations represented by this Note.

EXECUTED this _____ day of _____

[Borrower's Signature:]   *[Borrower's Printed or Typed Name]:*

In the sample documents above, some of the entries are filled in on the bill of sale and promissory note to give you a better idea as to how to fill in the form.

Miscellaneous in regards to closings

In continuing your professionalism. Always have extra pens, copies of documents and business cards or magnets to give to your buyer and seller.

I usually give my buyer two months to make the first payment. The buyer has enough to deal with financially during the month he moves in. So, I do not ask for payment until the second month after closing. This, again, makes me look like a hero and everyone is very excited about it.

County taxes on the mobile home may vary, but they are often under $500 a year. In Chicagoland area near where I live. I have seen them as low as $60 a year. These are not property taxes – those are included in the lot rent. The owner of the land (the park owner) pays the property taxes. The annual taxes paid on a mobile home come under different names depending on the county.

Whether you purchase the mobile home in your name, or an entity such as an LLC, realize that you will be paying taxes on the gains of the mobile home, when you sell the mobile home, not when the mobile home is paid off. So take the taxes you will be paying, on the gains of the mobile home, into consideration when you are calculating your Maximum Allowable Offer. Out of the gross profit, taxes on interest earned from your promissory note are going to be incurred. Out of the gross profit, capital gains taxes are going to be incurred (unless you buy the mobile home with a self-directed Roth IRA). Out of the profit, the expenses at the DMV will be paid as well as other miscellaneous expenses. All these expenses cut into your gross profit. Why is the mobile home title obtained at the Department of Motor Vehicles? Well technically, your mobile home is a vehicle, and technically you are buying and selling a vehicle. It has a Vehicle Identification Number (VIN). It has wheels. If you buy and sell too many vehicles, in your state, there may be a limit as to how many sales you are allowed before you are considered a mobile home dealer. You don't want to be mobile home dealer because there are many restrictions that are placed on you if you are a mobile home dealer and it can be very expensive. So find out how many mobile homes you can buy and sell each year in your own name, in your spouse's name, in the name of your LLC, in your IRA. You may have several entities through which you buy mobile homes. It is important to take note of how many sales you as an individual or entity are allowed without becoming a dealer in your state.

Creating a system for your closings is very important because it eliminates doubts for what to do. Go straight down your checklist so that you know you haven't missed anything. Your professionalism will show through, to all people that you're working with, in the closing. Those involved in the closing will be very impressed that you are so proactive and that you know what you are doing. You can even create a checklist for your buyer and seller if you wish. If you do so, there will be no doubts as to the procedure and his or her responsibilities at the closing.

Your checklist may look different. There may be different requirements at your motor vehicle department or your county office. There may be adjustments you need to make if your system does not exactly line up with your experience buying and selling a mobile home. Flexibility is the key. One motor vehicle department I worked with required that a police officer verify the VIN number on the mobile home, so that had to be arranged. But, that wasn't an issue. A glitch I came across, was when this motor vehicle department required the buyer to prove residency, in the state where the mobile home was located, in order for her to receive title to her mobile home. The buyer was planning on moving into the mobile home from another state. To prove residency in her new state, she needed to produce a utility bill from her address (her mobile home) where the vehicle to be registered (also her mobile home) was located. That was tricky, but we figured it out.

To receive documents in this chapter that you can print and use, check out the bonuses at this book's website:

www.thebookonincreasingyourroi.com

Now, all the paperwork has been exchanged and your buyer lives in her mobile home and all is well! But, it doesn't end there, because these are special people in your life. These are people you need to continue to nurture relational capital with. By relational capital, I mean continuing that sense of trust between you and the seller, you and the buyer, and you and the mobile home park. It is these little details that will be discussed in the next chapter, which will help you continue development of relational capital, and will ultimately allow you to obtain huge profits in the manufactured home market.

#9
ALL PARTIES WIN!
Who's In Need of feeling special? Everyone!

Learning about Finishing Touches that can Make Your New Client Feel Special and Brand You Favorably

Earlier, it was discussed how building trust between you and a buyer, or a seller or a park, increases relational capital. Relational capital is another way of expressing the good that comes from the development of good relationships. Good relationships mean good business. Good business means more profit. There are three key points in developing relational capital: communication, respect and professionalism. This book has discussed many different ways to communicate with the buyer, with the seller, and with the park. It is important to listen to the needs of each of these parties, because the more needs that are met, the more money you will make. Communication is really a key to growing your business. Keeping in touch with people who you have done business with, fosters repeat business and referrals. Respect is of the utmost importance. If you don't respect the person you are working with, he can tell, and he is not going to want to work with you. It is important to respect all of the people you are working with and show it. You do this with the words you choose to use and the way in which you choose to do business. Treat everyone you work with, with dignity and respect.

Professionalism sets the tone. As you can see from the closing procedure shown in the previous chapter, there is a very professional way to handle a closing. That professionalism is seen from day one. Your professionalism needs to show from the first moment that you answer the phone. If not, his trust will be eroded. There are too many scammers out there. For this reason, you need to appear as professional as possible, so that you are not viewed as just one of those other people trying to take money from the caller. That is certainly not what you are trying to do. Your purpose is to meet the needs of others.

How can you show the seller that she is really special, that you really do appreciate her? Well, besides purchasing the mobile home from her, which will mean quite a bit, you can listen to her and see what some of her other needs are. Undoubtedly, she needs some help with something. Maybe you can refer someone you know to help her. Listen to where she is coming from in case you can help her. If there is something she is interested in, that you enjoy as well, suggest an activity that you participate in. Tell her how much you enjoy it. Connections are the seeds of relational capital. When these grow, these develop into a relationship of trust. Trust goes both ways. Through trust, you will see all the needs that can be met. If you can fulfill those needs, you will both benefit in some way.

Again, I am not saying that you should be nosy, or that you should pry or even try to be her best friend, but the more interest you show in your seller, the more she sees that she is a person important to you, not just a sale. She will appreciate you more and be more likely to send you referrals or even repeat business. Just always be listening and ask yourself, "What more can I do for my seller?" And again, that communication, that listening, is really important. Earlier I talked about a seller who needed siding for his house. I was able to provide that. Other sellers had need of other references that I was able to share. Some were actually interested in pursuing real estate. So I suggested coming to my monthly Cash Flow game night. Sometimes reaching out with cards or phone calls, just to let your seller know you are thinking about her, without being annoying of course, is appreciated.

Sometimes, just showing an interest in the neighborhood, where the buyer used to live before moving, helps connect you to the buyer on an emotional level. An example of keeping communication open was when one of my buyers for a mobile home had problems with the roof and skylight long after she moved in. Actually, she was my second buyer to live in that mobile home since I bought it. I was able to talk to the original seller, who I had purchased the mobile home from. She was able to give me an answer of when it was last repaired and what had been done, so that the new owner was then able to proceed with the repair, with this background knowledge.

What can you do to make your buyer feel special? For starters, treating her with respect from the day she calls you about purchasing a mobile home. At closing, give her a list of utilities and insurance information and other information that will help her transition into her mobile home. I always send flowers and/or a gift card one week after closing, and I give the buyer a call to find out how everything is going and to see if there is anything I can help her with. You may choose to do this or something different.

Occasionally, I will send cards on holidays, or other times that I think are appropriate. Sometimes, I see whether a buyer has something that she wants to share with me; for example, one of my buyers really loves to garden. So in the spring and summer, I go over there to chat and look at her garden. She is so appreciative and thanks me again for helping her get this mobile home, which she hadn't thought she could ever be in.

Professionally, I send a bill once a month to each buyer who has a loan with me, so both of us have a record as to the status of the note.

Sometimes a buyer will call you because she is concerned about something that is happening in her mobile home. If a buyer calls with a concern, for example, "There's no water running in my mobile home". You don't say, "Too bad, you own the home, deal with it." At this point you know enough about repair situations with mobile homes, to know what questions to ask. The buyer may not know what questions to ask, and that is why it's nice she can talk to you. In this situation, I would first have the owner call the park, in order to see if the water main in the park is being repaired and perhaps she "didn't get the memo". Secondly, if it's winter, I would talk to her about heat tape. Are those raccoons biting into the heat tape again? Are those skunks nesting by the warm pipes? If the heat tape is manual, did the owner turn it on? Did it stop working? Does the mobile home have heat tape on its pipes? If needed, I can recommend a repair man, but I do not own the home, nor am I responsible for it. But I can be nice and helpful by directing the owner on how to solve the problem. By treating her with this kind of respect, I am more likely to get a referral from her. The buyer should feel like she is more than just a paycheck to you. Respect breeds respect and referrals.

How do you develop relational capital with the parks? Don't just call the park up to see what they have for you; find out what you can do for them. Can you refer people, who do not fit into your parameters, to their park? It's important to keep communication open with the park. What if you have an issue with your buyer not paying on time? Contact the park. Let them know that there is an issue. They may be having the same issue. If this issue is dealt with on two fronts, your buyer is likely to turn around what they are doing, or both of you can speak to the buyer and see what you can work out.

What can you do to increase relational capital with your investors? Don't treat your investor like a bank. Again, communicate with your investor, take an interest in him. Now it may be that he just wants to be a bank to you, but when you call him, ask: "How is life treating you? How are the kids? How is your dog?" Take an interest in his life without coming off as overbearing. Investing in you is helping him lead a better life. He is an essential part of your team. Keep your investor happy, so that you can have repeat business with him. Of course getting the investor the returns he desires is the key to getting repeat business, but making him feel like he is more than someone you are just getting money from, is important too.

Even the handymen and women who come to help you with your mobile home are important to have relational capital with. When a handyman is not working for you, give him other referrals. You may have heard someone needs a roofer. Pass on the name of your roofer. The other day someone mentioned to me that she needed a painter. I had just hired a painter a couple of months ago for exactly what this person needed, so I referred the painter to her. If you can refer your handyman to people and treat him, not just as a contractor, but someone who is an essential part of your team, then more than likely, when you need that contractor, he will be there for you.

There are many people you come in contact with every day, in your business, in your neighborhood, at the grocery store, at church, on an airplane, at family get-togethers and many other places. Everyone you meet is valuable. What life adventures lies hidden in the woman standing in front of you at the grocery store? Did she serve in the military in Iraq? Was she up all night with a dying parent? What about the man at the bus stop? Did he lose his fortune during the recession? Does he volunteer helping adults learn to read many hours a week? Or your neighbor whose passion for animals and the out of doors has him quietly volunteering at the local forest preserve and wildlife center on the weekends. Or the teen who stands in line at the amusement park, who dreams to become an Olympian. Unless you talk to him, he is just a person in line. Talking to, listening to, respecting and connecting with the people in your life is essential, not just because it is a good business practice, but because it gives you a fuller, richer life. What can you learn from all the people in your life? What can they learn from you? When you open your heart to others, people will open their heart to you. That kind of connection takes relational capital to a whole new level. It is kindness; it is compassion; it is love. It allows you to win in ways you cannot imagine. This is the way strong communities are built: learning from each other, helping each other, supporting each other, and building each other up. That is what you do in this business.

What steps can you take to forward your business and build a stronger community? Strong communities are not built in a day. It depends on the strength of a person like you. You have the dedication and commitment. Just by reading this book, you have taken a step forward. You are not alone. You will learn from others. You will grow in knowledge. You will meet other investors that will strengthen you.

This may sound like a lot to do, but given all the things that you need to take care of, and the people you need to make feel special, you should not forget to take care of yourself. Make yourself feel special too! Make sure you are rewarding yourself each step of the way as you climb higher and higher in this business. Set goals and reward yourself for your achievements. Reward your little goals, like finding a qualified buyer, by taking yourself out for ice cream. For medium goals, like completing your first transaction, reward yourself by going out to dinner and a movie. For large goals, like completing so many transactions per month, reward yourself by attending a professional sporting event or getting away for the weekend at a resort. Maybe one of your goals is to have enough cash flow to lease a BMW. Reward yourself. Of course, you don't want to eat up all the profits rewarding yourself. Don't forget, you are in this business to make money.

The best advice I recently received on this subject was given by someone who said to me, "Create the rules that make you succeed." And that is what you need to do. This book contains a system for success in the manufactured home market. Your system might ultimately be different than mine. But having a basis, having a foundation, having a beginning is important. For without a beginning, you will never start to WIN! Establish this well, and you will WIN! As other investors see your success, they will want to invest in you. You will increase your ROI. While everyone else is dealing with low interest rates in the bank, vulnerable stock markets or risky real estate deals, take advantage of this little known niche market and

WIN!

For a "to do" list on how to do a Mobile home deal from start to finish, check out the bonuses for this book:

www.thebookonincreasingyourroi.com

#10
More WINners! YOU CAN BE A WINNER TOO - OR WIN BY INVESTING IN ONE

These investors from other parts of the U.S. are also doing deals, buying and selling mobile homes

Christy Duckett-Harris, Jim Stehlik and Jim Jones are investors I have met in my journey.

Their successful deals described below do not necessarily use the same system as I have talked about in this book, but they use several of the techniques mentioned in the book.

Most importantly, Christy, Jim S., and Jim J. continue to receive payments month after month by selling mobile homes on terms with seller finance.

In the Examples below take note of the following:

- Check out Christy's phenomenal ROI!
- In both deals a buyer was found on craigslist.
- Check out the negotiating in Jim's deal.

- Notice that Christy used a credit card to buy her mobile home deal.
- Christy also takes note of the area surrounding the park. It is important that the mobile home be in a desirable neighborhood.
- Jim found that "no" did not mean "no" as far as purchasing mobile homes in the park. After completing the deal described below, he helped the park out more by rehabbing 3 more mobile homes, once the park management could see he was a professional and knew what he was doing. Note Jim bought those homes for $1.
- Note, Christy did over 15 deals in one park!

EXAMPLE ONE:

Name of investor: Christy Duckett-Harris from Columbia, SC.

Location of mobile home: The mobile home was purchased in West Columbia, across from Lexington medical hospital, in a very desirable area, down from the bus line and 5 minutes from downtown Columbia. The mobile home was built in 1994.

Christy's total out of pocket expenses, including the mobile home, moving the mobile home and repairs: $3100.

To purchase the home, Christy wrote a check provided by her credit card, which had 0% interest for the first 12 months.

Mobile Home:	$1500
Relocating Mobile Home:	$1100
Repairs	$500
Buyer purchased home for	$11,500
Down payment:	$1000

Loan Terms: $10,500 at 15.038% for 60 months at a $250/month payment.

Found Buyer: on Craigslist.
Found Seller: The seller responded to bandit sign: "WE BUY MOBILE HOMES."

The owner had built a new single family house, while living in the mobile home, and needed it moved off of the land. Christy and her team moved it into a park.

<u>Park Relationship</u>: Christy said: "We have a great relationship with that park owner and have filled the park with over 15 mobile homes."

<u>ROI on this deal:</u>
Total revenue is: $250 X 60 = $15,000
plus $1,000 down payment = **$16,000**;
initial investment = $3,100.

$$\frac{\$(16,000 - 3,100)}{\$3,100} = \frac{\$12,900}{\$3,100} = 4.16 = 416\% \; ROI$$

EXAMPLE TWO:
Investors: Jim Jones /Jim Stehlik. Stafford, VA
Mobile Home location: Woodford, VA

Seller was asking $7500. Jim offered $1000. The deal was negotiated at $2160

Jim paid cash for the purchase and rehab, total cost: $16,000

<u>Repairs</u>: Total gut rehab. New siding, all new floors, subfloor, vinyl, carpet, appliances, paint.

Buyer purchased price: $25,000
Down payment: $5000

Loan terms: $20,000 @$475/month for 48 month at around 6% interest.

Found Buyer: on Craigslist - Only one ad.
Found Seller: driving around mobile home parks.

Park Relationship: "At first the park was standoffish. They didn't want to allow the purchase. We talked a few times. They relented to allow this one rehab. Since then, they have sold us three more trailers at $1 each". Subsequent purchases at this park were done with IRA lenders found at a local REIA.

ROI on this deal:
Total revenue is: $475 X 48 = $22,800
plus $5,000 down payment = **$27,800**;
initial investment = $16,000.

$$\frac{\$(27,800 - 16,000)}{\$16,000} = \frac{\$11,800}{\$16,000} = 0.74 = 74\% \, ROI$$

About the Author

Lori Robinson, the author of *The Book on Increasing your ROI: How to Obtain Huge Profits in the Manufactured Home Market,* lives in Aurora, Illinois, USA, with her husband, Dean, and their cat Roxanne. They have three grown children, Heather, Brittany and Steve, who are in their 20s just beginning their own paths in life.

Lori's passion for community service along with her desire to run a profitable business came together when she discovered the manufactured home market, where she saw that her desire to help others could also earn high returns. She named her company Phoenix Home Enterprises with the idea that she could bring a new beginning to people's lives through a new home. People she has placed in mobile homes have often shown gratitude to the point of tears, thankful that they each had a place of his or her own at a monthly payment each could afford. These experiences gave Lori the incentive to continue to expand this aspect of her Real Estate business.

She wrote this book not only to point out the great need for so many hard working Americans to find decent affordable housing, but to show that in providing a solution to this housing need, one can not only positively impact lives but earn a high return on investment, up to and beyond doubling an initial investment in about 4 years!

Education is the key to informed investing. Lori feels that before investing money in anything, a person should understand what one is investing in, how one's money is being invested and who is impacted by these investments. In her book, she meticulously illustrates the answers to these and other concerns about investing in the manufactured home market. After reading this book, she hopes you will want to invest in the manufactured home market too. As a former educator, Lori knows that one approach does not fit all, but with the right tools and right approach, success is possible. Lori offers coaching and mentoring programs through her company to jumpstart those who want a hands-on approach to this business.

Most Americans who invest have some money in mutual funds. What impact do investments in these funds have on the investors' local community or even the community at large? Probably, none. Lori has seen that investing in the manufactured home market can provide better returns than the typical mutual fund portfolio and at the same time have a positive impact on people's lives. For those investors who want a hands-off approach to investing in manufactured homes, Lori offers, through her company, the opportunity to invest in individual manufactured homes.

Do you want to increase your ROI? Of course you do. Who wants investments with returns barely higher than inflation or worse? Whether you wish to be a hands-on or hands-off investor in the manufactured home market, Lori can help you succeed.

You can contact Lori by email: lori@callthephoenix.net

For more information and extra bonuses check out:

www.thebookonincreasingyourroi.com

www.ingramcontent.com/pod-product-compliance
Lightning Source LLC
Chambersburg PA
CBHW061315220326
41599CB00026B/4887